Secure Shell in the Enterprise

Jason Reid

Sun Microsystems Press
A Prentice Hall Title

The publishers offers discounts on this book when ordered in bulk quantities. For more information, contact: Corporate Sales Department, Phone: 800-382-3419; Fax: 201-236-7141; E-mail: corpsales@prenhall.com; or write: Prentice Hall PTR, Corp. Sales Dept., One Lake Street, Upper Saddle River, NJ 07458.

Production Supervision: *Mary Sudul*
Acquisitions Editor: *Gregory G. Doench*
Cover Design Director: *Jerry Votta*
Cover Designer: *Kavish & Kavish Digital Publishing and Design*
Manufacturing Manager: *Alexis R. Heydt*
Marketing Manager: *Debby vanDijk*

Sun Microsystems Press:
Publisher: *Myrna Rivera*

1st Printing

ISBN 0-13-142900-0

Sun Microsystems Press
A Prentice Hall Title

Acknowledgements

This book would not exist without the labor and skill of Dan Barnett. He kept me on track and met every request.

I am indebted to my technical reviewers: Kaustubh Desai, Scott Howard, Neal Kuhn, Darren Moffat, Alex Noordergraaf, Erik Swanson, Gaurav Shrivastav, Marco Walther, Markus Zellner, and the denizens of #security and security-interest. Their comments, suggestions, and criticisms have helped make this a better book.

Thanks to Alex Noordergraaf, Gary Rush, and Keith Watson for setting me on the path to writing this book.

Thanks to Neal Kuhn and Doug Smith for allowing me the time to write the book.

Thanks to the following people who have provided expertise and support to this book: Glenn Brunette, Valerie Bubb, Stephen Gillis, Bernd Guettler, Darren Moffat, Alec Muffett, Alex Noordergraaf, Laurent Pirotte, Brad Powell, Scott Rotondo, Andrew Sydelko, Marco Walther, Keith Watson, Joel Weise, and especially the Solaris System Test group.

Thanks to Monica French for her support and understanding while I was writing the book.

Finally, I would like to thank my family and friends.

Contents

Figures

Tables

Preface

This book is part of an on-going series of books collectively known as the Sun BluePrints™ program. *Secure Shell in the Enterprise* details best practices for facilitating and managing Secure Shell technology on the Solaris™ Operating Environment.

Sun BluePrints Program

The mission of the Sun BluePrints Program is to empower Sun's customers with the technical knowledge required to implement reliable, extensible, and secure information systems within the datacenter by using Sun products. This program provides a framework to identify, develop, and distribute best practices information that applies across the Sun product lines. Experts in technical subjects in various areas contribute to the program and focus on the scope and usefulness of the information.

The Sun BluePrints Program includes books, guides, and online articles. Through these vehicles, Sun provides guidance, installation and implementation experiences, real-life scenarios, and late-breaking technical information. The monthly electronic magazine, Sun BluePrints OnLine, is located on the Web at `http://www.sun.com/blueprints`. To be notified about updates to the Sun BluePrints Program, please register on this site.

Who Should Use This Book

This book is primarily intended for readers who will be deploying and integrating Secure Shell software into their computing environments. Detailed examples of configuring, deploying, and integrating OpenSSH and the Solaris™ Secure Shell software are provided, in combination with explanations of tradeoffs and problems encountered.

Before You Read This Book

For a nontechnical treatment of cryptography, refer to *The Code Book* by Simon Singh. For a technical treatment of cryptography with sample implementations, refer to *Applied Cryptography: Protocols, Algorithms, and Source Code in C* by Bruce Schneier. For the mathematics of cryptography, refer to *Cryptography and Data Security* by Dorothy Denning, *Basic Methods of Cryptography* by Jan C. A. Van Der Lubbe, or *Crytography: Theory and Practice* by Douglas Stinson.

To fully use the information in this document, you must have knowledge of the topics discussed in these books:

- *Solaris System Administration Guide: Basic Administration*
- *Solaris System Administration Guide: Advanced Administration*
- *Solaris System Administration Guide: Security Services*

Caution – The use of cryptographic tools is strictly regulated or even prohibited in some parts of the world. You should seek advice from your legal counsel before deploying, using, or exporting cryptographic software.

How This Book Is Organized

Chapter 1 provides an overview of the history of security as it applies to the Internet and enterprises, a description of security policies, a description of security tools, a discussion of security tool choices, and a description of the consequences of tool choices.

Chapter 2 provides information on how to build OpenSSH. It includes detailed discussions of the needed components, entropy sources, TCP Wrappers, and OpenSSL.

Chapter 3 provides information on how to configure the Secure Shell software. It includes detailed discussions of the needed configuration files, and configuration recommendations.

Chapter 4 provides information on how to deploy the Secure Shell software. It includes detailed discussions of packaging the software, generating MD5 hashes, using the Solaris Security Toolkit, and distributing custom configuration files.

Chapter 5 provides information on how to integrate the Secure Shell software into your environment. It includes detailed discussions of scripting the Secure Shell software, using proxies, integrating role-based access control and port forwarding, and disabling insecure services.

Chapter 6 provides information on key management. It includes detailed discussions of host keys, user identities, and agents.

Chapter 7 provides procedures on how to configure auditing so that you can audit system wide events and specific commands, how to enable and disable auditing, how to audit the system and specific users, and how to enable logging. It also includes information about OpenSSH auditing, cron(1M), workarounds, and patching.

Chapter 8 provides information on performance and sizing. It includes detailed discussions of bandwidth performance, symmetric ciphers, identity generation, and performance problems.

Chapter 9 includes case studies on virtual private networks and linking networks through a bastion host.

Chapter 10 provides information on problems, patches, and solutions.

Appendix A provides basic information on using the Secure Shell software, along with examples of client usage and server usage.

Appendix B provides a list of server configuration options.

Appendix C provides a list of client configuration options.

Appendix D provides a discussion of the methodology used in the performance and sizing tests discussed in Chapter 8.

Appendix E includes examples of the code and scripts used in the book and sample configurations for the client and server.

Appendix F provides references to Secure Shell documentation, software resources, and web sites.

Bibliography contains references to Sun BluePrints OnLine articles, external articles, books, bug reports, FAQs, man pages, and presentations that were used to write *Secure Shell in the Enterprise*.

Using UNIX Commands

This document does not contain information on basic UNIX® commands and procedures such as shutting down the system, booting the system, and configuring devices.

Refer to one or more of the following for this information:

■ *Solaris Handbook for Sun Peripherals*

■ AnswerBook2™ online documentation for the Solaris operating environment

■ Other software documentation that you received with your system

Typographic Conventions

Typeface	Meaning	Examples
AaBbCc123	The names of commands, files, and directories; on-screen computer output	Edit your .login file. Use ls -a to list all files. % You have mail.
AaBbCc123	What you type, when contrasted with on-screen computer output	% **su** Password:
AaBbCc123	Book titles, new words or terms, words to be emphasized. Replace command-line variables with real names or values.	Read Chapter 6 in the *User's Guide*. These are called *class* options. You *must* be the superuser to do this. To delete a file, type rm *filename*.

Shell Prompts

Shell	Prompt
C shell	*machine-name*%
C shell superuser	*machine-name*#
Bourne shell and Korn shell	$
Bourne shell and Korn shell superuser	#

Accessing Sun Documentation

You can view, print, or purchase a broad selection of Sun documentation, including localized versions, at:

`http://www.sun.com/documentation`

Sun Welcomes Your Comments

Sun is interested in improving its documentation and welcomes your comments and suggestions. You can email your comments to Sun at:

`docfeedback@sun.com`

Please include the part number (817-1024-10) of this document in the subject line of your email.

## CHAPTER 1

Introducing the Secure Protocols

The network has never been safe. As your data travels the network, it can be monitored, copied, or silently changed without your knowledge. Rogue users can hijack the connection to your mail server and read your corporate secrets. Physical console access is not practical when data centers are outsourced or when system administrators are on a separate continent. Thus, secure network connections are a business requirement for globally interconnected systems. Remote-access, cryptographic-protocol-based tools, such as Secure Shell or virtual private networks, were developed to defend against network security threats and to provide secure access.

Security History and Protocols

In the beginning, there was Telnet, and it worked. Users were able to log in remotely to machines across the Internet to check their email or to exchange files. The Internet was a small safe place built by and for academics. It was a place in which everyone knew everyone else, much like a small town. The focus was on accessibility and openness, not security. Where security was used, it was basically a simple screen-door latch, which could be easily bypassed.

Then the Internet exploded in size, reach, capacity, and population. Businesses started to use the Internet for commerce. Following the money and new arrivals, the criminals came. Screen-door latches were no longer enough protection. Telnet and FTP quickly failed because of their weaknesses (plaintext passwords, weak integrity, and lack of cryptography). Data was stolen, altered, or simply deleted. Tempered steel bank vaults were now needed to keep out the criminals. But the use of the old protocols had spread far and wide, and they had become standards that could not be changed. Together, the academics and the business people crafted new protocols and tools to lock down and secure their communications while maintaining compatibility with the base protocols.

Telnet, FTP, and the Berkeley r-commands are no longer safe ways of protecting your data and machines. However, there are replacements for these venerable protocols. Virtual private networks, Kerberos, Secure Shell, and IPsec are the new protocols that can secure your communications. The question now is which tool is right for your environment.

Secure Protocols

A secure protocol must address three concerns: establishing identity (authentication), protecting against tampering (integrity), and keeping the exchange private (confidentiality). The standard for communication on the Internet is the TCP/IP protocol suite, as defined by the Internet Engineering Task Force (IETF). TCP/IP uses a four-layer network stack in which each layer is separate and rests on the previous layer (TABLE 1-1). Each security concern must be handled at some point in the stack.

TABLE 1-1   Four-Layer TCP/IP Stack

Layer	Example
Application	Telnet and HTTP
Transport	TCP and UDP
Internet	IP
Network access	Ethernet

Authentication

Authentication means demonstrating that you are who you say you are. After you state your identity, either to your corporate mail server to retrieve your email or to the ticket agent behind the counter to pick up your airline tickets, how do they verify you are who you say you are? Verification is accomplished by one of three methods:

- Stating a known identifier—preferably secret, such as a password—or having a name matched to a list

- Displaying a unique, difficult-to-forge object, such as a token card or passport

- Letting a machine take a biometric measurement, such as a fingerprint or photograph, and compare it with a known sample

Some facilities require only one method of authentication. More secure facilities might have redundant methods. A popular and secure method is two-factor authentication, which involves using something the user has and something the user knows. A common format is a cryptographic challenge-and-response token, coupled with a user secret, such as a personal identification number (PIN). For example, before withdrawing money from an automatic teller machine (ATM), you must insert your token (ATM card) and share a secret (your PIN) to access your account. One factor without the other is useless—neither the PIN nor the ATM card alone will gain access to the account. Some ATM machines require a fingerprint scan, in instead of a PIN or in conjunction with a PIN.

Unfortunately, most systems (for instance, UNIX) use the traditional user name and password scheme. History has shown this to be a poor method for authentication. The problem is that passwords have typically been limited to eight or fewer characters. To be effective, the password must be cryptic and difficult to guess. Users prefer something that is easily remembered. They tend to use *sekret*, *password*, their spouse's name, their pet's name, or something else that is easily remembered. Thus, they tend not to use stronger choices like I4jk6Gh2, r00tb4m3, or tOaS15jk. Automated password-guessing tools like Crack make short work of poor passwords by using dictionary word lists of common passwords. The following is an example of weak authentication:

```
hook /home/suzi $ telnet blackbeard
Trying 192.168.10.200...
Connected to blackbeard.
Escape character is '^]'.
login: suzi
Password: sekret
Last login: Sat Oct  5 16:15:43 from hook
Sun Microsystems Inc.    SunOS 5.9        Generic May 2002
blackbeard /home/suzi $
```

Passphrases are a dramatic improvement over short passwords. Users will have a much easier time remembering a private fact about themselves or a loved one, such as *at 5, I 8 muuud with Suzi* or *carbon8 hydrogen10 nitrogen4 oxygen2*. Passphrases still need to be chosen carefully to avoid common phrases such as popular Shakespeare quotes. For example, *to be or not to be* is a poor passphrase. However, *2b or!b suffer ropes with rocks and pointy objects* is stronger because the quotation has been mangled.

Anything the user knows, such as passwords or passphrases, can, and probably will, be written down by the user, particularly when the user is faced with having a different password or passphrase for each system requiring authentication. A strong passphrase written down and carried by the user is arguably stronger than a weak password that the user can remember. Educate users to guard their authentication information and to not leave passwords and passphrases on small notes attached to their monitors or in their desks.

Before users are authenticated, they authenticate the provider. Returning to our earlier example, how do you identify an appropriate ATM? How do you know whether it is a real ATM from your bank or a fake ATM designed to harvest account and PIN numbers? You base your decision on labeling (for instance, colors and logos), placement, and history. You trust the corner grocer ATM that has served you for years. You may not immediately trust the oddly colored ATM that recently appeared in your shopping mall.

On the Internet, authentication gets murky. Packets from the host you want or an imposter impersonating that host (called spoofing) appear the same. When Suzi uses Telnet to connect to blackbeard, how does she know that she is getting blackbeard, and not an imposter? With standard name services, such as the domain name service (DNS) or network information services (NIS), you do not know because you have no guarantee that you received a legitimate answer to your name service request. You must initially take it on faith that you are communicating with the intended host. You could check later for some unique identifier, such as a file on the machine, but by then, your password has already been compromised.

This is where public key cryptography helps. It can be used in the protocol (IP) layer or in the application layer to identify machines. A common form is the certificate used to identify organizations (normally, the web server) engaged in electronic commerce. The certificate is issued by some authority that first verifies the organization's identity.

Integrity

When you receive a letter from someone, how do you detect accidental tampering (for example, rain smearing the ink) or malicious tampering (for example, someone adding words to change the meaning of the sentences)? You examine the letter, looking for damage or handwriting that does not match.

Network packets are ephemeral. They have no physical shape or form, so they cannot easily be inspected for damage. Network protocols use cyclic redundancy checks (CRCs) and hashes to detect damage. A hash is a mathematical function providing some representation of the data. Before a packet is transmitted, the data is hashed to produce CRCs that are transmitted with the data. When the packet is received, the receiver hashes the data and compares it to the stored CRCs. If the CRCs match, all is well. If not, a response is sent stating that the packet was corrupted in transit.

The hash functions for the TCP/IP layers were designed to be fast and computationally cheap. They worked well to detect random corruption by electrical noise, bad connections, or failing components in the network. However, they failed when faced with deliberately forged packets. A secure hash function must be one-way and collision free. If your field is too small, an equally valid data segment can be generated or the data can be altered and still produce a given checksum value. Examples of secure hash functions are MD5 and SHA-1.

Confidentiality

Authentication and integrity depend on confidentiality. Confidentiality means keeping the details of the communication private between the parties. Computer networks are best viewed as individuals talking in a public forum. There is no way to prevent or detect illicit recording of conversations. Cryptography ensures confidentiality.

The base TCP/IP protocols transmit in the clear because no cryptography is used for privacy. Such transmissions allow the disclosure of any password or passphrase, no matter how cryptic. Integrity is limited because any packet can be silently replaced. Cryptography hides the passphrases and hashes. If an attacker modifies a packet, the recipient discards it as invalid because the correct hash cannot be generated. Examples of cryptographic algorithms include Blowfish and RSA.

In the following example, the authentication (that is, login and password) for a Telnet session were transmitted in the clear.

```
# snoop blackbeard
Using device /dev/hme (promiscuous mode)
        hook -> blackbeard      TELNET C port=38630
        blackbeard -> hook      TELNET R port=38630
   .
   .
   .

        blackbeard -> hook      TELNET R port=38630 \377\373\1\377\375\1login:
        hook -> blackbeard      TELNET C port=38630
        blackbeard -> hook      TELNET R port=38630
        hook -> blackbeard      TELNET C port=38630
        hook -> blackbeard      TELNET C port=38630 suzi\n
        blackbeard -> hook      TELNET R port=38630 suzi\r\n
        hook -> blackbeard      TELNET C port=38630
        blackbeard -> hook      TELNET R port=38630 Password:
        hook -> blackbeard      TELNET C port=38630
        hook -> blackbeard      TELNET C port=38630 sekret\n
        blackbeard -> hook      TELNET R port=38630
```

Cryptographic Protocols

All of the cryptographic protocols—virtual private networks, IPsec, Kerberos, and Secure Shell—use the mathematics of cryptography to solve the authentication, integrity, and confidentiality problems.

Asymmetric ciphers, symmetric ciphers, pseudorandom number generators, and one-way functions (cryptographic hash functions) are the building blocks to produce a cryptographic protocol. Asymmetric ciphers, also known as public key ciphers, solve the authentication problem by using sets of keys to identify machines and users. Because of their superior performance over asymmetric ciphers, symmetric ciphers provide confidentiality for bulk encryption. Pseudorandom number generators are the entropy sources to seed the ciphers. Cryptographic hash functions detect tampering of the session and preserve integrity.

In the Telnet session example, had the user been using Secure Shell, none of the session traffic or the authentication details would be visible. A packet sniffer would see only gibberish as the data. The following is a Secure Shell session fragment. The fragment is from the beginning of the session.

```
       hook -> blackbeard      TCP D=22 S=51068 Push Ack=2912590257
Seq=1639940859 Len=52 Win=48296
        0: 0000 0c07 ac00 0800 20f9 0fb0 0800 4510    ........ u....E.
       16: 005c f2e4 4000 4006 27a6 8192 49a0 8192    .\..@.@.'...I...
       32: d33c c77c 0016 61bf 82fb ad9a 99b1 5018    .<.|..a.......P.
       48: bca8 fb4f 0000 1a70 553d db05 b9a6 e470    ...O...PU=.....p
       64: 9af4 2def 00e9 74cb a161 77db 2105 4207    ..-...t..aw.!.B.
       80: 3b40 a50d c191 3924 caec f078 c9ae 50a8    ;@....9$...x..P.
       96: 7f82 5903 01b9 f164 c3f3                   ..Y....d..

       blackbeard -> hook      TCP D=51068 S=22 Push Ack=1639940911
Seq=2912590257 Len=52 Win=48784

        0: 0800 20f9 0fb0 00d0 03f1 d7fc 0800 4500    .. u..........E.
       16: 005c 174c 4000 3a06 094f 8192 d33c 8192    .\.L@.:..O...<..
       32: 49a0 0016 c77c ad9a 99b1 61bf 832f 5018    I....|....a../P.
       48: be90 88e3 0000 7b30 4059 9990 a6b0 1c93    ......{0@Y......
       64: 8c60 45ac 0732 ac18 0584 4f86 870a 7d12    .`E..2....O...}.
       80: 9fc1 95c1 23b5 a4c3 d8a6 1525 7e35 50ef    ....#......%~5P.
       96: 14b7 978c 7921 e849 94dc                   ....y!.I..
```

Adding cryptography does not remove all of the problems. The math is only one piece of the puzzle. The cryptographic protocols protect your communications only in transit. They provide protection against sniffing, hijacking, spoofing, and tampering. They do not defend against users who choose weak passwords, firewalls that are not configured, or databases that allow connections (even if they are secure) to any machine on the Internet.

In any security solution, you must consider the people who have authorized access, the hardening of machines, and mistakes. People are the weakest link in any system. They get sick, forget, act inconsistently, make mistakes, and can be too helpful. If users are not educated to prevent disclosure of their passwords, passphrases, or any other confidential materials, no technical solution will help. An attacker can have easier access to data by entering the building with the assistance of an overly helpful employee than by defeating a firewall. You must educate your users. Give them the information they need to protect themselves and the company. Warn them of the consequences, but do not scare them into submission. Teach them that security is the responsibility of every employee, not just some distant support group.

Using cryptographic protocols on an unhardened machine is useless. If a machine has unnecessary services or is unpatched, an attacker can run the exploit-du-jour and gain access. No passwords are needed, and there is no cryptography to break. The rule of thumb is to turn off anything you would not give away. For example, if the machine is not a boot server, it should not have the `tftpd` daemon running. If something must be turned on, limit its communication. For example, the corporate database server needs to talk only to the database application front ends, not to any other client that connects to the network. The Solaris™ Security Toolkit software is an excellent starting point for hardening systems that use the Solaris Operating Environment (Solaris OE). You can find information about the Solaris Security Toolkit software on the Sun BluePrints program web site at:

`http://www.sun.com/security/jass`

For more information on hardening systems, refer to the following Sun BluePrints OnLine articles:

- "Minimizing the Solaris Operating Environment for Security: Updated for the Solaris 9 Operating Environment," November 2002, by Alex Noordergraaf
- "Solaris Operating Environment Minimization for Security: A Simple, Reproducible and Secure Application Installation Methodology Update for the Solaris 8 Operating Environment," November 2000, by Alex Noordergraaf

Everyone makes mistakes, including system administrators. The hardware and software must be correctly installed to be effective. Poor installations are at best a waste of time and money, and at worst, they are a security vulnerability. An unconfigured firewall is only slowing down the network. Before installing and configuring the hardware and/or software, read the product documentation. It warns about problems. Consider having another employee check the critical parts of the computing infrastructure. It is not an insult to the person who did the initial work; it is a safety check to catch problems before they become critical.

Remember to defend in depth. Never have just one lock in front of something sensitive. Use firewalls to limit network access. Use a cryptographic protocol solution such as IPsec or Secure Shell software to access the machine. Then, have a second authentication to access the corporate payroll application. The more serious the consequences of misuse or disclosure, the more significant the protection should be.

Security Policy

Risk cannot be eliminated, but it can be minimized. Management should establish a security policy based on the risks it is willing to take, depending on business, legal, regulatory, and technical factors. The policy consists of the rules and regulations that employees are expected to follow. The policy must be implementable, enforceable, and understandable, and it must be documented and distributed.

A policy does not specify the technical implementation. It is the instrument that states whether or not something is required and how it is to be generally configured. For example, the policy does not describe the configuration of a firewall to block port 80 (HTTP traffic). The policy simply states the requirement that Web traffic be blocked at the network perimeter.

In creating a security policy, management balances the risks versus the benefits of certain actions. The costs and probability of loss must be balanced against the cost of prevention. For example, the cost of data loss and downtime is weighed against the cost of an uninterruptible power supply (UPS). For a single large database server, management may decide to order a UPS and have it installed. For a thousand end-user workstations, management may decide the cost is too high.

A good security policy should answer the following questions:

- What needs to be protected?
- What levels of protection should be provided?
- How often are software versions checked?
- How often are machines patched?
- When are new versions upgraded?
- Who is authorized access to what?
- How are information and machines to be disposed of at the end of life?
- How is the policy audited?

A policy is only as good as its auditing or ongoing validation. If no one ever checks that the rules are being followed, employees will stop following them when it is expedient to do so. Audits also give management a measurement of the costs of prevention. Based on the audit conclusions, management may decide that the cost of prevention is too high or too low.

If you do not have a security policy, consider establishing one. The policy will guide the configuration of any solution you deploy. Your internal audit or risk management department may already have the requirements. For smaller sites, a variety of information is available on the Internet. For more information, refer to the following Sun BluePrints Online articles:

"Developing a Security Policy," December 2001, by Joel Weise and Charles R. Martin

"Responding to a Customer's Security Incidents—Part 1: Establishing Teams and a Policy," March 2003, by Vijay Masurkar

"Responding to a Customer's Security Incidents—Part 2: Executing a Policy," April 2003, by Vijay Masurkar

Tools

You have documented the security threats and explained the potential for damage to your management. Management has examined the risks and has decided to require protection of the company's communications. Now comes the technical decision of which tool to use. The tools decision is based on the following factors:

- Are you protecting only internal traffic, such as files on an NFS home directory server?
- Do you have legacy applications to protect?
- How varied are the platforms to be supported?
- Do you need remote access for employees who travel or for those who work from home?

In this section, four choices are examined: Kerberos, IPsec, virtual private networks, and Secure Shell.

Kerberos

Kerberos was developed at the Massachusetts Institute of Technology (MIT) as part of the Athena Project that investigated distributed computing during the 1980s. The Athena Project sought to provide strong authentication and, optionally, confidentiality. Kerberos works by having a master server, called the key distribution center, pass out tickets that are the user's credentials when accessing a service. A ticket contains information about the user's identity and a temporary encryption key.

In a Kerberos environment, there is no need for employee retraining. Employees use *kerberized* replacements of unsafe commands such as Telnet. Kerberos is well suited to local environments in which a number of workstations and servers need their traffic protected.

The weaknesses of Kerberos involve the key distribution center (KDC) being a single-point-of-failure, applications needing to be converted to use Kerberos, and clock drift. The following list contains explanations of these weaknesses:

- The KDC contains all of the passwords. If the KDC is compromised, an attacker can impersonate any user. The KDC becomes a single-point-of-failure in this regard. The KDC absolutely must be hardened to prevent this situation.

- Before a user can use an application, it must be converted to use Kerberos. If the source is not available or the vendor is unwilling to convert the application, it may not be possible to use the application safely.

- In the handling of tickets, the KDC and the requesting application machine's clock must be within a certain time range (normally, five minutes). If the clocks differ more than that, the tickets will not be considered valid. In corporate networks in which the clocks can be controlled by the network time protocol (NTP), clock drift is not a problem. With machines that experience only intermittent network connectivity, such as laptops, clock drift may prevent authentication.

The current Kerberos protocol (version 5) is documented in RFC 1510 (RFCs are available at `http://www.ietf.org/`). Additional information can be found at the following locations or in the following documents:

- MIT Kerberos web site at:

  `http://mit.edu/kerberos/www/`

- `comp.protocols.kerberos` FAQ at:

  `http://www.nrl.navy.mil/CCS/people/kenh/kerberos-faq.html`

- "Kerberos Network Security in the Solaris Operating Environment" (Sun BluePrints Online, October 2001) by Wyllys Ingersoll, at:

  `http://www.sun.com/blueprints/`

- Sun Microsystems's Kerberos web site at:

  `http://www.sun.com/software/security/kerberos/`

- Security Services section of the *Solaris 9 9/02 System Administration Guide* at:

  `http://docs.sun.com/`

- SEAM(5)

IPsec

IPsec was developed to solve the problems of authentication, integrity, and confidentiality in the base networking protocols, thus freeing applications from any protocol concerns. IPsec allows for centralized policy control and is transparent to both users and applications. It supports both IPv4 and IPv6.

IPsec has become the industry-standard method for securing network connections, when available. It is often the underlying basis for virtual private networks. Its weakness is its lack of universal support. Legacy versions of the Solaris OE and many non-UNIX-derived operating systems do not support IPsec. IPsec is integrated into Solaris OE versions 8 and 9. The Solaris 9 OE also provides Internet key exchange (IKE) support. The Solaris 8 OE is limited to manual keying only.

IPsec is documented in RFCs 2401, 2403, 2404, 2405, 2406, 2407, 2408, 2409, 2410, 2411, and 2451. Additional information can be found in the following documents:

- "IPSec in the Solaris 9 Operating Environment" technical white paper at:

  `http://wwws.sun.com/software/whitepapers/solaris9/ipsec.pdf`

- IP Services section of the *Solaris 9 9/02 System Administration Guide* available at:

  `http://docs.sun.com/`

- `ipsec(7P)`

Virtual Private Networks

Virtual private networks (VPNs) are about building secure tunnels through untrusted networks. In the beginning, VPNs were used to link corporate network segments over inexpensive Internet connections, using a proprietary protocol rather than expensive leased lines. Eventually, VPNs expanded to provide connectivity from remote clients, such as laptops, into the corporate network. VPNs allow for centralized policy control and are transparent to applications.

The weaknesses of VPNs stem from the VPN gateway being a single-point-to-attack, traffic being protected only in the tunnel, and the physical network view being replaced by the virtual network view. The VPN gateway is the funnel through which traffic passes. Compromise it, and all of the connections are compromised. Traffic is protected only while it is in the tunnel. After traffic leaves the VPN gateway, it is in the clear and subject to the usual forms of attacks. Network maintenance is increased because the network must be viewed in terms of both its physical connections and the virtual connections created by the tunnels.

Secure Shell

The Secure Shell software was originally created by Tatu Ylönen. His implementation was a drop-in replacement for Telnet, FTP, and the Berkeley r-commands (rlogin, rsh, rexec, and rcp). Like its insecure counterparts, the Secure Shell is a client-server application. A Secure Shell server awaits connections. When a connection is initiated, the server identifies itself by using its public host key and the version of the protocol it expects. The problems of authentication, integrity, and confidentiality are solved in the application layer by the Secure Shell protocol. No changes to the standard TCP/IP protocols are required, so interoperability is maintained. The current level of the protocol is 2. Version 1 has been deprecated because weaknesses were found in its design. The Secure Shell is a fully distributed system with no centralized policy control.

Note – The name Secure Shell refers to both the protocol and the implementation of the protocol.

Being a drop-in replacement, Secure Shell requires minimal employee retraining for basic use. Simply replace the old command names with their Secure Shell counterparts. Telnet or rsh becomes ssh, rcp becomes scp, and ftp becomes sftp. More advanced use, such as protection of the WebNFS™ file system or HTTP traffic, requires some knowledge of TCP sockets. Secure Shell works very well for system administrators needing a secure connection to their Solaris OE machines.

The weaknesses of Secure Shell are its distributed nature and lack of transparency to users and applications. There is no central point of control. This requires configurations and keys to be distributed to all machines. Large-scale installations quickly become awkward. The advantage of Secure Shell is that there is no single-point-of-failure to attack. One endpoint of every connection must be compromised to break the encrypted traffic. Before applications can be protected (that is, tunneled), they must be individually configured to use the tunnel. Novice users may not be capable of setting up this configuration.

The Secure Shell software is integrated into the Solaris 9 OE. Commercial and free implementations are available for other Solaris OE versions and for non-Solaris OE platforms. The Secure Shell protocol, version 2, is documented in the following Internet draft documents:

- "SSH Transport Layer Protocol"
- "SSH Authentication Protocol"
- "SSH Connection Protocol"
- "SSH Protocol Architecture"
- "Generic Message Exchange Authentication for SSH"
- "GSSAPI Authentication and Key Exchange for the Secure Shell Protocol"

- "Diffie-Hellman Group Exchange for the SSH Transport Layer Protocol"
- "SSH Agent Forwarding"
- "SSH Fingerprint Format"
- "SSH Protocol Assigned Numbers"
- "Using DNS to Securely Publish SSH Key Fingerprints"

Some of these drafts are available at:
`http://www.ietf.org/html.charters/secsh-charter.html`

Additional information about Secure Shell can be found in the following Sun documents:

- Security Services section of the *Solaris 9 9/02 System Administration Guide* at:

  `http://docs.sun.com/`
- `ssh(1)`
- `sshd(1M)`

Determining Which Tool to Use

To determine which tool to use for your environment, use the following decision tree.

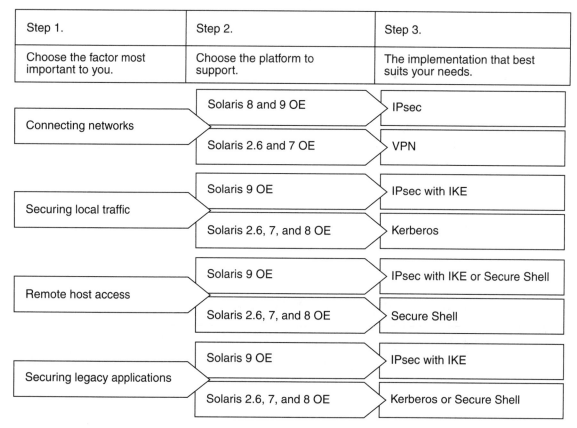

Step 1.	Step 2.	Step 3.
Choose the factor most important to you.	Choose the platform to support.	The implementation that best suits your needs.
Connecting networks	Solaris 8 and 9 OE	IPsec
	Solaris 2.6 and 7 OE	VPN
Securing local traffic	Solaris 9 OE	IPsec with IKE
	Solaris 2.6, 7, and 8 OE	Kerberos
Remote host access	Solaris 9 OE	IPsec with IKE or Secure Shell
	Solaris 2.6, 7, and 8 OE	Secure Shell
Securing legacy applications	Solaris 9 OE	IPsec with IKE
	Solaris 2.6, 7, and 8 OE	Kerberos or Secure Shell

FIGURE 1-1   Tool Decision Tree

Tool Decision Example A

You want to connect a remote sales office in Akron, Ohio, to the main office in Dresden, Germany. You want the sales office network to appear as part of the main network. The gateways at both ends are running the Solaris 7 OE. You should select a VPN solution, such as the SunScreen™ 3.1 software.

Tool Decision Example B

Your system administrators require remote access to the web server farm to repair faults. All of the servers are running the Solaris 9 OE. You should select a Secure Shell solution. Use the Solaris Secure Shell software on the servers and an appropriate implementation for the clients.

Secure Shell Choices

If a Secure Shell solution is right for your enterprise, you can choose from a variety of implementations. Because of the client-server nature of the protocol, the client and the server can use different implementations on disparate architectures (for example, PuTTY on a Windows 2000 IA-32-based machine connecting to the Solaris Secure Shell software on a Solaris 9 OE SPARC®-based machine). The choice of which implementation to use depends on three factors: platform availability, support, and cost.

Solaris Secure Shell Software

The Solaris Secure Shell software is included only in the Solaris 9 OE release. It supports Solaris OE features such as the SunSHIELD™ Basic Security Module (BSM) and internationalization, and support is available from Sun Microsystems, Inc. The Solaris Secure Shell software supports versions 1 and 2 of the Secure Shell protocol.

OpenSSH

OpenSSH is the most popular server implementation and focuses mostly on UNIX platforms. It arose out of a disagreement the OpenBSD group had with SSH Communications, Inc., about the licensing of the original Secure Shell implementation. OpenSSH supports a number of platforms, including Linux and the Solaris OE. OpenSSH is provided under a BSD-style license. Consult the `LICENSE` file in the OpenSSH distribution for more information. OpenSSH supports versions 1 and 2 of the Secure Shell protocol. No commercial support is available, but a Usenet news group and mailing list offer community support.

Noncommercial Implementations

Most non-UNIX implementations tend to be client only. Clients range from PuTTY, by Simon Tatham, for the Microsoft Windows platforms to Top Gun SSH for the PalmOS platform. Before deployment, check the license under which the software is distributed, and confirm that version 2 of the Secure Shell protocol is supported. Commercial support is not available, and community support has ceased for some of the software versions.

The Netscape™ Communications Corporation's Open Directory Project has a list of clients available at:

```
http://dmoz.org/Computers/Security/Products_and_Tools/
Cryptography/SSH/Clients/
```

Commercial Variants

F-Secure, SSH Communications, and Van Dyke Software are a few of the companies providing commercial Secure Shell implementations. Commercial variants tend to support non-UNIX platforms for clients, and commercial support is generally available. The Open Directory Project link given above also lists commercial clients.

Determining Which Secure Shell Software to Use

To determine which Secure Shell software to use for your environment, use the following decision tree.

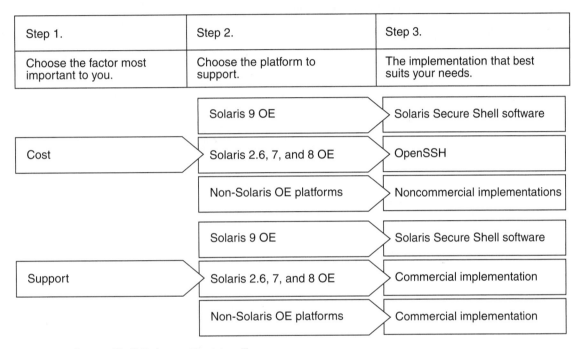

Step 1.	Step 2.	Step 3.
Choose the factor most important to you.	Choose the platform to support.	The implementation that best suits your needs.

Cost
- Solaris 9 OE → Solaris Secure Shell software
- Solaris 2.6, 7, and 8 OE → OpenSSH
- Non-Solaris OE platforms → Noncommercial implementations

Support
- Solaris 9 OE → Solaris Secure Shell software
- Solaris 2.6, 7, and 8 OE → Commercial implementation
- Non-Solaris OE platforms → Commercial implementation

FIGURE 1-2   Secure Shell Software Decision Tree

Secure Shell Software Decision Example A

You have a number of Microsoft Windows XP-based laptops and a single Solaris 9 OE server to support. Support is your largest concern. For the laptops, choose a commercial implementation and purchase support. For the server, choose the Solaris Secure Shell software so that you will have one service provider for both the hardware and software on the server.

Secure Shell Software Decision Example B

You want to automate content distribution on your Solaris 8 OE Web farm. The content is pushed from one central server to the farm. You decide community support is good enough and want a low-cost solution. Choose OpenSSH.

Consequences

Cryptographic protocols are not a panacea. With their usage come the drawbacks of past insecurity realization, changes to a new system, and some loss of control. If you are using insecure protocols, you may have already been compromised. The last thing to do is to panic and quickly throw together a secure solution. A hastily deployed solution will be a sloppy solution with wasted time, wasted money, and heightened emotions.

Some solutions have serious issues with key management. If you throw keys around in an unsafe manner, you will have only the appearance of security because the communications will be compromised. Knowing your weaknesses and mitigating them is superior to a false sense of security. Do the job correctly the first time, and you will not have to patch it again and again.

People are resistant to change, particularly when it means a new way of doing things that inconveniences them. Explain the new solution to the users (IT customers). Educate them, and show them why it is necessary. Show how the old method can harm them and the company. Educate them, but do not scare them into submission.

Cryptographic protocol tools such as Secure Shell have both advantages and disadvantages. The tools can secure your connections from prying eyes, and they can prevent an intruder from penetrating the corporate database server and retrieving credit card numbers from the e-commerce application back end. In addition, the Secure Shell can secure communication channels from automated attack agents and provide back doors into compromised machines. However, cyptographic protocols blind network intrusion detection and auditing systems. From a network view, you know only that someone is doing something, not whether he or she is uploading a presentation or downloading contraband.

## CHAPTER 2

Building OpenSSH

OpenSSH is a free, BSD-style license, implementation of the Secure Shell protocols. OpenSSH is designed for strong authentication, for improved privacy, and for secure X11 sessions. OpenSSH is developed on and for the OpenBSD operating system by the OpenBSD group. The OpenSSH portability team then transforms the OpenBSD version into the portable version that supports many UNIX-derived operating systems, including the Solaris OE and the Linux operating system.

Components

Several components must be present before you can build OpenSSH. These components must either be installed individually or as part of the Solaris OE. The following components are needed:

- Solaris OE build machine
- `gzip`
- ANSI C compiler
- Perl
- Zlib
- Entropy source
- TCP Wrappers (optional)
- OpenSSL
- OpenSSH

See "Resources" on page 181 for information on how to obtain the individual software components.

The instructions in this book use software package names and file names that do not reference the version number of the software packages. Always use the latest versions. The instructions were written using the following specific versions:

- Solaris 9 OE for SPARC processors
- gzip 1.3 (included with the Solaris 9 OE)
- Forte™ Developer 7 C 5.4 (rebranded as Sun™ ONE Studio 7, Compiler Collection)
- Perl v5.6.1 (included with the Solaris 9 OE)
- Zlib 1.1.4
- /dev/urandom (Solaris 9 OE feature and entropy source)
- PRNGD 0.9.26 (entropy source)
- TCP Wrappers 7.6
- OpenSSL 0.9.6g
- OpenSSH 3.5p1

Consult the installation documentation to prevent build problems.

Before Building OpenSSH

Before you build OpenSSH, you must consider the issues discussed in this section. Compiling code is output intensive. The build and compiler output are not included in the examples.

Static Versus Dynamic Libraries

Zlib, OpenSSL, and TCP Wrappers can be built as either static or dynamic libraries. The default is static. The advantage of static libraries is better performance and integration. A statically linked binary is faster to start up, and the executable can be installed as a standalone component. It depends on no supporting libraries (other than the required system dynamic libraries such as libc.so). The disadvantage is that changes to a static library require replacing and relinking the executable. Dynamic libraries allow just the library to be replaced and the program restarted. For this reason, the Solaris OE 8 and 9 versions ship only dynamic libraries. Unless you foresee the need to replace libraries frequently, use the default of static libraries. This simplifies the configuration, build, and deployment process.

Install Versus Build Location

OpenSSH requires its components to be installed in the `/usr/local` directory for building. On the deployed machines, OpenSSH can be installed in the `/opt/OBSDssh` directory, the `/usr/local` directory, or some other location. You must choose the location before building because the location is compiled into the executables.

About $PATH

The component configure scripts expect the programmer (developer) utilities in the `/usr/ccs/bin` directory to be in the $PATH environment variable. If `/usr/ucb/bin` is in the $PATH variable, it must be located after the compilers and the programmer utilities directory to prevent the wrong `cc` command from being called.

Checking MD5 Hashes and GNU Privacy Guard Signatures

Before you build the software packages, verify that they have been downloaded correctly by either checking their GNU Privacy Guard (GPG) signature or MD5 hash. If either differs from the original, do not use the package. You can obtain the MD5 software at:

`http://sunsolve.sun.com/md5/md5.tar.Z`

The compressed TAR file contains both SPARC and x86 binaries. Note that the file permissions on the extracted binaries must be changed to executable. Consult the GNU Privacy Guard documentation for instructions on building GPG and checking signatures.

Component Descriptions

This section describes the OpenSSH components.

Solaris OE Build Machine

The build machine must have the same base architecture as the targeted deployment machines. The Solaris OE is currently available for two platforms: SPARC and x86. You can check the architecture by using the uname(1) command with the -m option. If you deploy both platforms, you will be required to build OpenSSH twice, once for each architecture.

The following table will help you determine which build machine architectures are compatible.

TABLE 2-1   OpenSSH Compatible Architectures Examples

Build Architecture	Target Architecture	Comments
Ultra 1 SPARC	Netra™ T1 SPARC	These architectures are compatible.
Ultra 1 SPARC	LX-50 x86	These architectures are not compatible.
LX-50 x86	LX-50 x86	These architectures are compatible.
LX-50 x86	Sun Fire™ 15K SPARC	These architectures are not compatible.

Solaris OE Release

You must build OpenSSH on the oldest Solaris OE release that you plan to support. Newer releases of the Solaris OE are backward compatible. To maintain compatibility across releases, you might not be able to use new features of the Solaris OE. Building a single package reduces build-time costs and prevents a wrong package from being installed. You can check the release version with the uname(1) command.

Metaclusters

The build machine must have one of the following metaclusters installed:

- SUNWCprog (developer metacluster)
- SUNWCall (entire Solaris OE distribution)
- SUNWCXall (entire Solaris OE distribution plus OEM support)

The programmer utilities located in the /usr/ccs/bin directory are required to build OpenSSH, and /var/sadm/system/admin/CLUSTER contains the metacluster software installed on the machine. If the metacluster is not one of the three listed above, the build machine will need to be reinstalled with the correct metacluster.

Caution – Do not build OpenSSH on the intended deployment machines. This caution is particularly critical for machines installed with a minimized approach. Building the software requires a compiler and interpreters that could provide leverage for an attacker. Build the software and package it on the build machine, then deploy it to other machines.

Gzip

The component source software packages are distributed in the Gzip format (for example, *package_name*.tar.gz). The file must be uncompressed before it can be extracted. Neither uncompress(1) nor unzip(1) will be able to uncompress the file. Gzip comes with the Solaris 8 and 9 OE releases. For previous releases, you will have to download the Gzip software and build it from the source. Alternatively, prebuilt binaries can be downloaded at:

http://www.sunfreeware.com/

Compilers

An ANSI C-compliant compiler is needed to build the various components. Either the Forte C or GNU C compiler will work. Forte C has the advantage of being able to produce more highly optimized executables, particularly with the relevant flags being used. The optimization flag usage becomes a factor when you are building the math-intensive OpenSSL cryptographic library. The Forte compiler has the disadvantage of being a separate product. Consult your sales representative for more information on obtaining it. The GNU compiler, gcc, is available free of charge.

Note – Make sure the build system has the appropriate patches applied. This is especially important if you are using the Forte C compiler.

To build gcc, refer to its documentation. To obtain prebuilt versions of gcc, go to:

http://www.sunfreeware.com/

Perl

You will need version 5 of the Practical Extraction and Reporting Language (Perl) to configure and install OpenSSL and OpenSSH. Perl version 5 comes with the Solaris 8 and 9 OE releases. For previous releases of the Solaris OE, you must download Perl and build it from the source. To obtain prebuilt binaries, go to:

```
http://www.sunfreeware.com/
```

Zlib

Zlib is a lossless data-compression library. Zlib is needed for compilation of OpenSSH. Optionally, OpenSSH also uses Zlib to compress data as it is transmitted and received to reduce bandwidth consumption. Zlib comes with the Solaris 8 and 9 OE releases in dynamic library form.

Note – As stated in Sun Alert 43541, users of Solaris 8 OE systems should apply the Zlib patch (patch ID 112611 for SPARC and 112612 for x86). The Zlib patch fixes a security bug detailed in CERT Vulnerability VU#368819.

For the Solaris 2.6 and 7 OE releases, Zlib will need to be built to statically link OpenSSH or for minimized machines without the Zlib dynamic libraries. To build a dynamic Zlib library, consult the documentation.

Note – Do not use versions before `zlib-1.1.4` because they contain an exploitable vulnerability.

▼ To Build Zlib

- To configure Zlib to use the Forte C compiler:

1. **Change the** `zlib-x.x.x` **directory.**

2. **Use the** `env(1)` **command to set the options and execute the** `configure` **script.**

```
$ env CC=cc \
CFLAGS="-xO5 -xdepend -xprefetch -dalign -xlibmil -xunroll=5 " \
./configure
```

Note – If the target machines do not have an UltraSPARC® II or III processor, omit the `-xprefetch` flag.

---

3. Use the make(1S) command to build the Zlib software.

```
$ make
```

4. Use the make(1S) command to test the build.

```
$ make test
hello world
uncompress(): hello, hello!
gzread(): hello, hello!
gzgets() after gzseek: hello!
inflate(): hello, hello!
large_inflate(): OK
after inflateSync(): hello, hello!
inflate with dictionary: hello, hello!
                    *** zlib test OK ***
```

5. Install the Zlib software by executing the following commands:

```
$ su
Password: password
# PATH=/usr/ccs/bin:$PATH
# export PATH
# make install
# ls -l /usr/local/lib/libz.a
-rwxr-xr-x   1 root  other        104308 Oct 10 14:03 libz.a
```

- To configure Zlib to use the GNU C compiler:

1. Change to the zlib-*x.x.x* directory.

2. Execute the configure script.

```
$ ./configure
```

3. Use the make(1S) command to build the Zlib software.

```
$ make
```

4. Use the make(1S) command to test the build.

```
$ make test
hello world
uncompress(): hello, hello!
gzread(): hello, hello!
gzgets() after gzseek: hello!
inflate(): hello, hello!
large_inflate(): OK
after inflateSync(): hello, hello!
inflate with dictionary: hello, hello!
              *** zlib test OK ***
```

5. Install the Zlib software by executing the following commands:

```
$ su
Password: password
# PATH=/usr/ccs/bin:$PATH
# export PATH
# make install
# ls -l /usr/local/lib/libz.a
-rwxr-xr-x   1 root   other       104308 Oct 10 14:03 libz.a
```

Entropy Sources

Entropy is the measurement of available randomness. A source of randomness is needed to generate cryptographic keys. The keys cannot be predictable because an attacker would be able to guess the key and break the encryption. The problem is that computers are deterministic machines, so they are very unsuited to the task of random number generation. Computers can only produce pseudorandom numbers that are, at best, very close to random. True random numbers can only be generated with hardware that measures stochastic natural phenomena, such as radioactive decay.

Hardware-based random number generators are often expensive and have slow bit rates of entropy production. Instead, software-based pseudorandom number generators are used. Randomness is approximated by measuring a series of partially random events such as the timing between key strokes, mouse positions, or arrival of network packets. All of the entropy is collected into a pool and *stirred* (a mathematical process to improve randomness).

The standard interface for entropy requests is to provide two sources: random and urandom. The random source provides processed entropy from the pool. If the pool is empty or not enough entropy is present to fulfill a request, random source will block (wait until completion) until enough entropy becomes available. The urandom source provides processed entropy from the pool if available. If not enough entropy is available, a cryptographic hash of the available entropy is returned instead. The urandom source will never block.

The random source always provides the highest quality of entropy with the performance penalty of requests being nondeterministic. The urandom source avoids this penalty by providing lower-quality entropy when the pool is low. The interface can be implemented by two character pseudodevices, FIFOs, or UNIX domain sockets.

Use the following criteria to choose an entropy source for OpenSSH:

- The source supports the intended Solaris OE release (2.6, 7, 8, or 9)
- The source supports either 32-bit or 64-bit kernel mode
- The source supports the SPARC and Intel platforms
- The source is self-contained

Choose from the following entropy sources:

- OpenSSH internal entropy collection
- Kernel-level random number generator
- ANDIrand
- SUNWski
- Entropy-gathering daemon
- Pseudorandom number generator daemon

OpenSSH Internal Entropy Collection

If no other entropy source is provided at OpenSSH configuration time, then the internal entropy collection is used as the default. Upon the invocation of OpenSSH, entropy is gathered by user-level commands, such as ps(1). OpenSSH will block until enough entropy is gathered. This gives the appearance that OpenSSH has hung, particularly on lightly loaded systems. Internal entropy gathering is not recommended because of its poor performance.

Kernel-Level Random Number Generators

Kernel-level random number generators implement the standard entropy interface as two character pseudodevices: `/dev/random` and `/dev/urandom`. A kernel implementation has access to all internal state information such as process context and device driver intrinsics. The information provides a larger and finer-grained source of entropy than can be obtained from user-level sources. The Solaris 9 OE and the Linux operating system provide a kernel-level random number generator. With the Solaris 8 OE, the random number generator is provided in a patch (patch ID 112438 for SPARC and 112439 for Intel). Kernel-level random number generators are the recommended entropy source.

ANDIrand

`ANDIrand` is a kernel module developed by Andreas Maier to generate random numbers at the kernel level. It provides the `/dev/random` and `/dev/urandom` character pseudodevices. This module is not supported by Sun, so it is not recommended for systems requiring Sun support services.

SUNWski

`SUNWski` is a user-level daemon for the Solaris 2.6 OE. It provides the `random` entropy source interface as a FIFO special file. It is not available for other Solaris OE releases, so it is not recommended.

Entropy-Gathering Daemon

The entropy-gathering daemon (EGD) is a user-level daemon written in Perl by Brian Warner for GNU Privacy Guard. It provides only the `random` entropy source interface through a UNIX domain socket. This source will block, causing performance problems, so it is not recommended. EGD also requires the installation of `perl`(1), which is not recommended for minimized systems.

Pseudorandom Number Generator Daemon

The pseudorandom number generator daemon (PRNGD) is a user-level daemon written in C by Lutz Jaenicke. It provides both the `random` and `urandom` entropy sources through a UNIX domain socket. It conforms to the EGD protocol for entropy requests. PRNGD is recommended for systems without a kernel-level random number generator.

Recommendations

Whenever possible, use a kernel-level random number generator. It provides the highest quality of pseudorandom numbers. A kernel-level random number generator has access to the private state information in the kernel, and it is difficult for an attacker to determine the inner state. If you cannot use a kernel-level random number generator, use the PRNGD daemon. The following table contains entropy recommendations based on the operating environment.

TABLE 2-2 Entropy Source Recommendations

Solaris OE Release	Source
Solaris 9 OE	`/dev/random`
Solaris 8 OE	`/dev/random` (patch 112438 or 112439)
Solaris 2.6 or 7 OE	PRNGD

Building PRNGD Software

PRNGD must be configured manually because there is no configure script. Configuration and building occur at the same time. PRNGD does not need to be installed on the build machine because it is packaged later for deployment.

▼ To Build PRNGD With the Forte C Compiler

- For the Solaris 7, 8, or 9 OE:

1. **Change to the `prngd-x.x.x` directory.**

2. **Use the `make(1S)` command to build the software package.**

```
$ make CC=cc CFLAGS="-xO5 -DSOLARIS" SYSLIBS="-lsocket -lnsl"
```

- For the Solaris 2.6 OE:

1. Change the directory to the `prngd-x.x.x` **directory.**

2. Use the make(1S) **command to build the software package.**

```
$ make CC=cc CFLAGS="-xO5 -DSOLARIS26 -D__EXTENSIONS__" \
SYSLIBS="-lsocket -lnsl"
```

▼ To Build PRNGD With the GNU C Compiler

- For the Solaris 7, 8, or 9 OE:

1. Change to the `prngd-x.x.x` **directory.**

2. Use the make(1S) **command to build the software package.**

```
$ make CC=gcc CFLAGS="-O3 -DSOLARIS" SYSLIBS="-lsocket -lnsl"
```

- For the Solaris 2.6 OE:

1. Change to the `prngd-x.x.x` **directory.**

2. Use the make(1S) **command to build the software package.**

```
$ make CC=gcc CFLAGS="-O3 -DSOLARIS26 -D__EXTENSIONS__" \
SYSLIBS="-lsocket -lnsl"
```

Manually Installing PRNGD

To install PRNGD, you must perform the following four steps:

1. Installation of the software

2. Selection of the entropy commands configuration file

3. Creation of the entropy pool location

4. Generation of the initial seed

The PRNGD makefile does not provide for these steps, so installation must be done manually.

Note – Manually installing PRNGD is only necessary for testing. PRNGD installation and startup on client machines is handled by scripts, as described in "Deploying Secure Shell" on page 53.

▼ To Install PRNGD

1. **Change to the** `prngd-x.x.x` **directory.**

2. **Become the superuser.**

3. **Create the** `/usr/local/sbin` **directory, if needed.**

```
# mkdir -m 755 -p /usr/local/sbin
```

4. **Copy** `prngd` **to the** `/usr/local/sbin` **directory.**

5. **Change the owner and permissions on the PRNGD daemon.**

```
# chown root:bin /usr/local/sbin/prngd
# chmod 755 /usr/local/sbin/prngd
```

6. **Copy the configuration file to the** `/etc` **directory.**

```
# cp contrib/Solaris-7/prngd.conf.solaris-7 /etc/prngd.conf
```

7. **Create the** `/var/spool/prngd` **directory, and change the ownership.**

```
# mkdir -m 755 -p /var/spool/prngd
# chown root:bin /var/spool/prngd
```

8. **Use the following commands to generate the seed:**

```
# cat /var/log/syslog > /var/spool/prngd/seed
# ps -efl >> /var/spool/prngd/seed
```

Running PRNGD

As described in "Scripts and Configuration Files" on page 159, support for PRNGD in included in the OpenSSH init script. For systems without /dev/random, the PRNGD software is started before the OpenSSH daemon, sshd(1M), is started. Place the script in the /etc/init.d directory, then link it in /etc/rc3.d. You must run this script before any init script for OpenSSH.

▼ To Start the PRNGD Manually

1. Become the superuser.

2. Use the following command to start the daemon:

```
# /usr/local/sbin/prngd --cmdfile /etc/prngd.conf \
--seedfile /var/spool/prngd/seed /var/run/egd-pool
```

▼ To Stop the PRNGD Manually

1. Become the superuser.

2. Use the following command to stop the daemon:

```
# /usr/local/sbin/prngd --kill /var/run/egd-pool
```

Testing the Entropy Source

Testing the entrophy source depends on the source you are using. Testing involves checking for different results. This section contains instructions for checking /dev/random and PRNGD.

Checking /dev/random

You can do a simple check with the dd(1M) and the od(1) commands. Read a few bytes of data from the source, and convert it to a viewable form. Repeat the process a few times, and check that different results are returned. This is a not a statistically sound method, but it ensures basic functionality.

The following example shows how to check /dev/random:

```
$ dd if=/dev/random bs=4 count=1 | od -x
1+0 records in
1+0 records out
0000000 8e76 3ac8
0000004
$ dd if=/dev/random bs=4 count=1 | od -x
1+0 records in
1+0 records out
0000000 c495 2b37
0000004
```

Checking PRNGD

Checking PRNGD is a bit more difficult. It requires EGD protocol commands to request entropy. In "Scripts and Configuration Files" on page 159, you will find the C source to check PRNGD. It requests four bytes of entropy from the given PRNGD pool and displays them. Again, this is not checking the statistical functionality of the randomness. It is a basic sanity test. Repeat the check a few times to ensure that different values are returned.

The following example shows how to check PRNGD:

```
$ cc -o checkprngd checkprndg.c -lsocket -lnsl
$ ./checkprngd /var/run/egd-pool
69 -6 -72 19
$ ./checkprngd /var/run/egd-pool
119 -120 112 35
$ ./checkprngd /var/run/egd-pool
-4 -13 -19 -6
```

TCP Wrappers

TCP Wrappers provides limited, application-oriented, host-based firewall functionality with which connections can be denied or accepted based on the originating host. Connection attempts are logged using syslog(3C). OpenSSH uses this functionality by linking in the libwrap library. TCP Wrappers depends on the name and IP address information returned by the name services, such as DNS. It cannot stop low-level, network-based attacks, such as port scanning, IP spoofing, or denial of service. For those, a packet-based firewall solution such as the SunScreen software is necessary. The Solaris 9 OE includes TCP Wrappers (SFWtcpd, which is located in the /usr/sfw directory). For the Solaris 8 OE (starting in the Solaris 8 10/00 release), TCP Wrappers can be found on the Software Companion CD. For the Solaris 2.6 and 7 OE releases, TCP Wrappers must be downloaded and built from the source (see "Resources" on page 181). TCP Wrappers is not required for building OpenSSH.

Building TCP Wrappers

This section contains procedures for building the TCP Wrappers software.

▼ To Build TCP Wrappers

- For the Forte C compiler:

1. **Change to the** tcp_wrappers_x.x **directory.**

2. **Use the following command to build the TCP Wrappers software:**

```
$ make REAL_DAEMON_DIR=/usr/sbin sunos5 \
STYLE="\"-xO5 -xdepend -xprefetch -dalign -xlibmil -xunroll=5 \""
```

Note – If the target machines do not have an UltraSPARC II or III processor, omit the -xprefetch flag.

- For the GNU C compiler:

1. **Change to the** tcp_wrappers_x.x **directory.**

2. **Use the following command to build the TCP Wrappers software:**

```
$ make REAL_DAEMON_DIR=/usr/sbin sunos5
```

▼ To Install TCP Wrappers

TCP Wrappers does not have an automated install script. OpenSSH requires only two files from the distribution: libwrap.a and tcpd.h.

1. **Become the superuser.**

2. **Copy the** libwrap.a **file to the** /usr/local/lib **directory.**

3. **Copy the** tcpd.h **file to the** /usr/local/include **directory.**

4. Change the ownership and permissions with the following commands:

```
# chown root:other /usr/local/lib/libwrap.a /usr/local/include/tcpd.h
# chmod 755 /usr/local/lib/libwrap.a /usr/local/include/tcpd.h
```

OpenSSL

OpenSSL is a general-purpose cryptographic library that also implements the Secure Sockets Layer (SSL) protocol. This is the component that does all of the cryptographic work for OpenSSH.

Note – The OpenSSL library contains patented cryptographic algorithms; however, OpenSSH does not use them. The README file lists the patents that might apply. Consult your legal counsel as to whether or not this is an issue.

The config script attempts to build a library optimized for the specific build machine. This library is not distributable or portable, particularly if the build machine is not identical to the intended target machines. Instead, use the Configure Perl script to build a more general library. In selecting the designated support, choose the lowest common denominator platform.

TABLE 2-3   OpenSSL Configure Architecture Designations

Supported Architectures	Forte C Compiler	GNU C Compiler
sun4c, sun4d, sun4m, sun4u	solaris-sparcv7-cc	solaris-sparcv7-gcc
sun4d, sun4m, sun4u	solaris-sparcv8-cc	solaris-sparcv8-gcc
sun4u	solaris-sparcv9-cc	solaris-sparcv9-gcc
i86pc	solaris-x86-cc	solaris-x86-gcc

Avoid all of the designations in the following list:

- Designations that start with debug, for example, debug-solaris-sparcv8-gcc

  These will cause performance problems because they are meant only for debugging problems with the library.

- `solaris64-sparcv9-gcc31` or `solaris64-sparcv9-cc`

  These designations will not link with the 32-bit Zlib and OpenSSH components.

- `solaris-sparc-sc3`

  This compiler is not supported on the Solaris 2.6, 7, 8, or 9 OE releases.

▼ To Build and Test OpenSSL

1. **Change to the** `openssl-x.x.x` **directory.**

2. **Run the** `Configure` **script with the appropriate designation.**

```
$ ./Configure designation
```

3. **Use the** `make(1S)` **command to build and test the OpenSSL software.**

```
$ make
$ make test
```

▼ To Install OpenSSL

1. **Become the superuser.**

2. **Add** `/usr/ccs/bin` **to the** `$PATH` **variable, and export the variable.**

```
# PATH=/usr/ccs/bin:$PATH
# export PATH
```

3. **Use the** `make(1S)` **command to install the software.**

```
# make install
```

OpenSSH

OpenSSH is the OpenBSD group's implementation of the Secure Shell protocols 1 and 2. It is based on Tatu Ylönen's original Secure Shell implementation. Before building OpenSSH, all of the required and optional components must be built and installed on the build machine.

Configuring OpenSSH

The `configure` script includes many arguments that affect the compilation and installation process. OpenSSH must be configured based on the installation targets, compiler choice, and entropy source usage.

▼ To Obtain the List of Arguments in the `configure` Script

1. **Change to the** `openssh-x.xpx` **directory.**

2. **Execute the** `configure` **script with the** `-help` **option to obtain the argument list.**

```
$ ./configure -help
```

As a best practice, you should build OpenSSH with the following arguments:

- `--with-pam`

  This argument enables the use of pluggable authentication modules.

- `--disable-suid-ssh`

  To prevent a local `root` compromise if a vulnerability is found with the `ssh(1)` command, do not install OpenSSH with the `setuid` bit. The `setuid` bit is only needed for regression to the `rsh` protocol, which is disabled by the following option.

- `--without-rsh`

  This argument prevents the regression to the insecure `rsh` protocol if you are unable to connect by using the Secure Shell protocol.

- `--with-lastlog=/var/adm/lastlog`

  This argument defines the `lastlog` file location for the Solaris OE.

- `--sysconfdir=/etc/openssh`

This argument establishes the location for the OpenSSH configuration files. Make it a standard location, but avoid /etc/ssh to prevent a collision with the Solaris Secure Shell software. The location can also be: /etc or /usr/local/etc

- --prefix=/opt/OBSDssh

This argument establishes the top-level installation directory. The /opt/OBSDssh directory is for package generation. You can also use the /usr/local directory. The top-level installation directory is where OpenSSH looks for its various components.

- --without-privsep-user

This argument disables privilege separation due to pluggable authentication module interactions.

- --without-privsep-path

This argument also disables privilege separation due to pluggable authentication module interactions.

Note – The UsePrivilegeSeparation keyword must be set to no in the sshd_config file for the OpenSSH Secure Shell daemon to start. See "Configuring the Secure Shell" on page 41 for more details.

- --with-prngd-socket=/var/run/egd-pool

For systems using PRNGD, add this argument. It is the location of the entropy pool socket.

- --without-prngd

For systems using /dev/random without PRNGD, add this argument. Do not use PRNGD.

- --without-rand-helper

For systems using /dev/random, add this argument. Do not use the subprocess entropy gatherer.

Note – The configure script will report Random number source: OpenSSL internal ONLY; disregard this message.

- --with-tcp-wrappers=/usr/local

For TCP Wrappers support, add this argument. If you are using the integrated Solaris 9 OE version, use the /usr/sfw directory instead of the /usr/local directory.

- --with-cflags="-xO5 -xdepend -dalign -xlibmil -xunroll=5 - xprefetch "

For the Forte C compiler, add this argument.

Note – If the target machines do not have an UltraSPARC II or III processor, omit the -xprefetch flag.

▼ To Configure OpenSSH

- **Execute the command with the noted flags for the appropriate usage and compiler.**

  - For package creation, /dev/random usage, and the Forte C compiler:

```
$ ./configure --with-pam --disable-suid-ssh --without-rsh \
--with-lastlog=/var/adm/lastlog --sysconfdir=/etc/openssh  \
--prefix=/opt/OBSDssh --without-privsep-user --without-privsep-path \
--without-prngd --without-rand-helper \
--with-cflags="-x05 -xdepend -dalign -xlibmil -xunroll=5 -xprefetch "
```

  - For package creation, /dev/random usage, and the GNU C compiler:

```
$ ./configure --with-pam --disable-suid-ssh --without-rsh \
--with-lastlog=/var/adm/lastlog --sysconfdir=/etc/openssh  \
--prefix=/opt/OBSDssh --without-privsep-user --without-privsep-path \
--without-prngd --without-rand-helper
```

  - For package creation, PRNGD usage, and the Forte C compiler:

```
$ ./configure --with-pam --disable-suid-ssh --without-rsh \
--with-lastlog=/var/adm/lastlog --sysconfdir=/etc/openssh  \
--prefix=/opt/OBSDssh --without-privsep-user --without-privsep-path \
--with-prngd-socket=/var/run/egd-pool \
--with-cflags="-x05 -xdepend -dalign -xlibmil -xunroll=5 -xprefetch "
```

  - For /usr/local installation, PRNGD usage, and the GNU C compiler:

```
$ ./configure --with-pam --disable-suid-ssh --without-rsh \
--with-lastlog=/var/adm/lastlog --sysconfdir=/etc/openssh  \
--prefix=/usr/local --without-privsep-user --without-privsep-path \
--with-prngd-socket=/var/run/egd-pool
```

Building OpenSSH

Build OpenSSH by executing the make(1S) command, as in the following procedure. Installation is not needed because OpenSSH is packaged later for deployment.

▼ To Build OpenSSH

1. **Change to the** openssh-*x.xpx* **directory.**

2. **Execute the** make**(1S) command.**

```
$ make
```

## CHAPTER 3

Configuring the Secure Shell

Configuration is the the technical implementation of the local security policy. When setting the policy, management decided the level of protection needed for machines and data. Now you must implement their decisions when configuring Secure Shell. Secure Shell has a variety of options, some of which may not be appropriate to your local situation. Configure according to your policy. Again, if you do not have a security policy, it is important to establish one.

In configuring Secure Shell, keep in mind two principles:

- Defense-in-depth

  Let no single point of configuration or defense be the only gatekeeper for security.

- Plan on failure

  Secure Shell can, and should, be configured at multiple points (build-time, server configuration, and client configuration). No single misconfiguration should completely break the system security.

Example client and server configurations can be found in "Scripts and Configuration Files" on page 159. Consult the appendixes on server and client configuration options for information on individual options. Also refer to vendor documentation because the appendixes are not all encompassing. OpenSSH exists in a particularly fluid state with new options occasionally appearing.

Configuration Details

In order of precedence, Secure Shell configuration occurs at the following places: the software build-time, the server command-line options, the server configuration file (`sshd_config`), the client command-line options, the user client configuration file

(~/.ssh/config), and the global client configuration file (ssh_config). Build-time configuration is the strongest. It cannot be changed without rebuilding the software. This makes it inconvenient if a change is needed.

The server configuration involves the following: how the sshd(1M) daemon will present itself on the network, what protocols and authentication methods are acceptable, and how the user environment is constructed. The client configuration involves the following: determining which server to transact with which protocol, verifying the server identity, determining the user identity presentation, and choosing the ease-of-use features. Policy details are implemented on the server side. The client cannot override or provide a feature that the server does not offer.

The available features can be enabled or disabled by either command-line options or the applicable configuration file. Command-line options apply to a particular instantiation of either the server or client. Configuration file options are persistent until the file is altered and a new instantiation started. The most reliable configuration method uses the configuration file. This gives a repeatable, reproducible invocation. Changes can also be tracked by using source control. For information on command-line options, consult the vendor documentation.

Mechanics of Configuration Files

When OpenSSH is built, sshd_config and ssh_config are placed at the location specified by sysconfdir. Usual locations are /etc, /usr/local/etc, /etc/ssh, or /etc/openssh. The Solaris Secure Shell software stores the two files at /etc/ssh. These files should be owned by user root and group sys. The file permission mode should be either 644 or 444.

Configuration files contain two types of entries: comments and keyword-value pairs. Comments are blank lines and lines beginning with the hash mark (#). Keyword-value pairs consist of an identifier (keyword), a space, and the value associated with the identifier. Keywords are case insensitive, where as values are case sensitive.

Traditionally, the first letter of each word in a keyword is capitalized for readability. Some values are lists that are either comma delimited or space delimited, depending on the keyword. Consider keeping configuration files under source control to track revisions. The source control tags can be hidden by the comment character (the hash mark).

```
# Example config file - two comments and one
# keyword-value pair
Port 22
```

Recommendations

During configuration, you will need to make trade-offs between security, ease-of-use, and legacy compatibility. A wide variety of options covering network and protocol support, authentication, and user environment, obscure the individual option's impact on the whole. This section includes some configuration recommendations and discusses the consequences of their usage.

Note – Only the Solaris Secure Shell software and OpenSSH versions that are current at the time of this writing are used. Not all of the options are covered. Consult the vendor documentation for information on the other options and on the options presented here.

Server Recommendations

Server configuration specifies how the daemon presents itself on the network, what protocols are offered, and what authentication methods are allowed. Specific recommendations are given for each topic. Recommendations specific to a particular Secure Shell implementation have also been noted.

Protocol Support

Two major versions of the Secure Shell protocol exist. Protocol 1 has been deprecated because of vulnerabilities, such as packet insertion and password-length determination. Whenever possible, use Protocol 2. Unfortunately, many legacy clients support only Protocol 1. If this protocol must be enabled, consult the Legacy Support recommendations later in this chapter. Consider migrating to clients that support Protocol 2 as soon as reasonably possible.

Network Access

By default, the sshd(1M) daemon listens on all network interfaces on its bound ports. For workstations or other systems on which accessibility is desired for all interfaces, this behavior is not a problem. For architectures such as the Service

Delivery Network, in which management traffic is limited to a particular interface, this behavior is a problem. Limit network access with the ListenAddress keyword. Access is limited by a particular IP address, not by a network interface.

```
# Listen only to the management network.
ListenAddress 192.168.0.10
```

To further narrow down what the daemon will listen to, use either a host-based firewall, such as the SunScreen™ software, or TCP Wrappers.

For information about traffic-limited architectures, consult the Sun BluePrints OnLine article "Building Secure N-Tier Environments" (October 2000).

Keep-Alives

Occasionally, connections are temporarily suspended when a route is downed, a machine crashes, a connection is hijacked, or a man-in-the-middle attack is attempted. TCP keep-alives should be sent to detect any of these cases. If TCP keep-alives fail, the server will disconnect the connection and return allocated resources. Regular disconnects can aggravate users on faulty networks.

```
KeepAlive yes
```

Data Compression

Optionally, compression can be used on the encrypted data streams. This use results in bandwidth savings for compressible data, such as interactive logins or log files, at the expense of more CPU resources. For uncompressible data such as encrypted or compressed files, the extra CPU time is wasted and decreases performance. For a single Secure Shell session, these losses are inconsequential. For a file server, the extra load could impact performance. In this case, turn compression off to prevent misconfigured clients from driving up the system load.

```
# Transferring ASCII data such as interactive logins or log files
Compression yes
```

```
# Transferring random data such as compressed or encrypted files
# Prevents performance issues and reduces CPU load
Compression no
```

Privilege Separation

Privilege separation is an OpenSSH-only feature. The sshd(1M) daemon is split into two parts: a privileged process to deal with authentication and process creation and an unprivileged process to deal with incoming network connections. After successful authentication, the privileged process spawns a new process with the privileges of the authenticated user. The goal is to prevent compromise from an error in the network facing process. Unfortunately, privilege separation is not really compatible with pluggable authentication modules or SunSHIELD Basic Security Module (BSM) auditing. Some OpenSSH features are also disabled. If privilege separation is desired, consult the vendor documentation.

Note – The compilation options presented in Chapter 2 disable privilege separation.

```
# OpenSSH only
UsePrivilegeSeparation no
```

Login Grace Time

The default login grace time is the time a connection is allowed to exist before being successfully authenticated. The default of 600 seconds for the Solaris Secure Shell software and 120 seconds for later OpenSSH versions is too long. Reduce the time to 60 seconds.

```
LoginGraceTime 60
```

Password and Public Key Authentication

Passwords are not always appropriate. A stronger means may be required, such as public-key cryptographic two-factor authentication. Secure Shell refers to the key pair as an identity. See "Managing Keys and Identities" on page 71 for more details. When passwords are deemed sufficient, do not allow empty passwords. They are too easy to guess.

```
PasswordAuthentication yes
PermitEmptyPasswords no
PubKeyAuthentication yes
DSAAuthentication yes
```

Superuser (`root`) Logins

Neither the Solaris Secure Shell software nor OpenSSH honors the values set in the /etc/default/login file. To prevent network superuser (root) logins, they must be explicitly denied. The Solaris Secure Shell software and OpenSSH default to yes. However, the default sshd_config(4) file in the Solaris Secure Shell software disables this feature. This forces a system administrator to log in as an unprivileged user, then change users (su) to the superuser. Enable superuser logins only if the system has no user accounts and the appropriate host protection is in place.

```
PermitRootLogin no
```

Banners, Mail, and Message-of-the-Day

Some sites require that a banner be displayed after a user connects to a system, but before logging in. You can accomplished this with the Banner keyword. Set Banner to /etc/issue so that only one banner file exists for the entire system.

```
Banner /etc/issue
```

In the Solaris OE, the interactive login shell is expected to display the message-of-the-day (MOTD) and to check for new mail. With some versions of OpenSSH, this feature causes the MOTD display and mail check to be done twice. Set these keywords to no to eliminate the duplication.

```
CheckMail no
PrintMotd no
```

Connection and X11 Forwarding

Secure Shell can tunnel TCP and X protocol connections through encrypted connections established between the client and server. Tunneling the traffic is referred to as forwarding. The forwarding occurs at the application level and is not completely transparent to the applications being forwarded. The applications need some configuration to use the tunnel.

Note – Data is protected only while it is in the tunnel between the client and server. After that, it is normal network traffic in the clear.

Tunneled traffic bypasses firewalls and intrusion detection systems. Allowing connection (TCP port) forwarding allows remote users safer access to email or the corporate web server. X forwarding allows system administrators to run GUI applications remotely, such as the Solaris™ Management Console software. This may not be functionality you want your users setting up. You can inconvenience users by turning off the functionality, but as long as they have shell access, they can run their own forwarders. Use role-based access control to explicitly limit what you want your users to do in this case.

If port forwarding is enabled, disable `GatewayPorts` and notify your users. `GatewayPorts` allows machines, other than the client, to access the forwarded ports in the tunnel. This access effectively bypasses any firewall usage. Again, users could run their own private forwarders on their client machines to defeat the server restrictions. Consider placing an intrusion detection sensor on the private network side of a Secure Shell bastion host to detect problem traffic.

```
AllowTCPForwarding yes
GatewayPorts no
X11DisplayOffset 10
X11Forwarding yes
XAuthLocation /usr/X/bin/xauth
```

User Access Control Lists

User access control lists (ACLs) can be specified in the server configuration file. No other part of the Solaris OE honors this ACL. You can either specifically allow or deny individual users or groups. The default is to allow access to anyone with a valid account. You can use ACLs to limit access to particular users in NIS environments, without resorting to custom pluggable authentication modules. Use only one of the following four ACL keywords in the server configuration file: `AllowGroups`, `AllowUsers`, `DenyGroups`, or `DenyUsers`.

```
# Allow only the sysadmin staff
AllowGroups staff
```

```
# Prevent unauthorized users.
DenyUsers cheng atkinson
```

User File Permissions

If a user has left their home directory or .ssh files world writable either by accident or by trickery, an intruder could insert identities allowing password-free access or alter the known_hosts file to allow man-in-the-middle attacks. With StrictModes enabled, the sshd(1M) daemon will not allow a login. But, users can be easily confused because they will not know why they cannot log in. No different error message is presented to them.

```
StrictModes yes
```

If you decide to disable StrictModes, consider eliminating public-key-based authentication to prevent user account compromise. The consequence is the elimination of password-free logins for users or automated jobs.

UseLogin Keyword

For OpenSSH only, UseLogin specifies that the OpenSSH sshd(1M) call login(1) instead of performing the initial login tasks itself for interactive sessions. login(1) must be called for BSM auditing. Unless UseLogin is set to yes, cron(1M) will partially break if SunSHIELD BSM auditing is enabled. See "Auditing" on page 81 for details on the consequences of UseLogin and on getting BSM auditing to work successfully. UseLogin will not work if UsePrivilegeSeparation is enabled. Enabling UseLogin disables X11 and port forwarding.

```
UseLogin no
```

Legacy Support

If legacy clients must be supported, strengthen the default configuration as much as possible. Default to Protocol 2 for the clients that support it. Disable all of the rhosts-style authentication methods. Increase the server key size and decrease the ephemeral key regeneration interval to minimize offline factoring attacks against the keys.

```
# Enable protocol 1 but default to protocol 2.
Protocol 2,1
# Legacy support options - protocol 1 only
HostKey /etc/ssh/ssh_host_key
IgnoreRhosts yes
IgnoreUserKnownHosts yes
KeyRegenerationInterval 1800
RhostsAuthentication no
RhostsRSAAuthentication no
RSAAuthentication yes
ServerKeyBits 1024
```

Client Recommendations

Client configuration specifies host option assignment, data compression, keep-alives, protocol support, and identity management. Specific recommendations are given for each topic.

Host Option Assignment

Configuration options can be assigned to a specific host or to all hosts by using the Host keyword. The value is matched to what the user types on the command line, not to the actual host name of the server. An asterisk (*) is used to set global default options. Options assigned to a specific host have precedence over the global defaults.

```
# Only for a specific host
Host legacy
Protocol 1

# For all hosts
Host *
Protocol 2
```

Data Compression

Data compression can be used on the encrypted data stream to save bandwidth. Set to off by default, you should enable it for interactive sessions or for transferring easily compressible data. The compression cost is asymmetric in that compressing the data is more computationally expensive than decompression. Client-side CPU cycles are generally cheaper than server-side CPU cycles. Avoid attempting to compress already compressed or encrypted data to avoid needlessly raising the CPU load on the server.

```
# For interactive sessions, low bandwidth links, or easily
# compressable files
Compression yes
```

Keep-Alives

Enable TCP keep-alives to detect downed connections. See "Keep-Alives" on page 44 for the server recommendations.

```
KeepAlive yes
```

Protocol Support

Always use Protocol 2 when possible. See "Protocol Support" on page 43 for the server recommendation.

```
Protocol 2
```

rlogin and rsh

The rlogin and rsh protocols should not be used. Prevent the client from attempting to execute rsh if a Secure Shell connection is refused.

```
FallBackToRsh no
UseRsh no
```

Server Identity

Verify server identity both by its host key and IP address. For higher levels of identity assurance, set `StrictHostKeyChecking` to `yes` and distribute host keys out-of-band. This is impractical when users frequently encounter new hosts. Set `StrictHostKeyChecking` to `ask`, and train the users to verify the offered host key with the stored host key on the server. See "Managing Keys and Identities" on page 71 for more information.

```
CheckHostIP yes
# only access one host
StrictHostKeyChecking yes
```

```
CheckHostIP yes
# access a variety of hosts
StrictHostKeyChecking ask
```

User Identity

User identities are stronger and provide more flexibility than does password authentication. When user identities are combined with agents, password-free logins can safely be obtained if the server permits it. See "Integrating Secure Shell" on page 59 and "Managing Keys and Identities" on page 71 for details.

```
DSAAuthentication yes
PubkeyAuthentication yes
```

## CHAPTER 4

Deploying Secure Shell

Automating and standardizing the installation of Secure Shell enables efficient rollouts, easier integration into existing environments, and reduction of maintenance. This chapter complements the Building OpenSSH chapter by explaining how to create and deploy an OpenSSH software package. Using the JumpStart™ technology, automated OpenSSH installations can be performed, along with automated configuration of both OpenSSH and the Solaris Secure Shell software.

OpenSSH Deployment

Efficient distribution requires that all of the OpenSSH components (client, server, configuration files, and documentation) be combined into a single entity, either a TAR file or, preferably, a System V package. TAR files are easy to create and transfer, but they require manual installation. System V packages are the standardized process for installing, updating, and removing software on the Solaris OE.

The components of the Solaris OE are installed using packages. A package enables automated installation of OpenSSH, as needed or at install time, using the JumpStart software technology. The binaries, configuration files, and documentation are copied to their respective locations, and any needed symbolic links are created.

For more information on packages, refer to the *Application Packaging Developer's Guide* at http://docs.sun.com and to the following man pages:

- pkgadd(1M)
- pkginfo(1)
- pkgmk(1)
- pkgparam(1)
- pkgproto(1)

- pkgtrans(1)
- installf(1M)
- pkgask(1M)
- pkgrm(1M)
- removef(1M)

OpenSSH Packaging

The makeOpenSSHPackage.ksh script creates a Solaris OE package. It takes the OpenSSH executables, configuration files, documentation, and optionally, PRNGD's executables and configuration files, and creates the OBSDssh package. The packaging script configures the openssh.server init script that is based on its own configuration.

The OpenSSH Tools TAR file is available on the Sun BluePrints Online, Scripts and Tools Web site. This TAR file contains the makeOpenSSHPackage.ksh packaging script, the openssh.server script, PRNGD test program source code, and client and server configuration examples. You can obtain the TAR file at:

http://www.sun.com/blueprints/tools/index.html

The makeOpenSSHPackage.ksh script uses the sshd_config.out file and the ssh_config.out file as the default configuration files for the OpenSSH installation. Place your local configuration into these files before generating the package.

The OBSDssh package does not generate host keys at install time. Keys are generated at first boot to prevent hosts installed by WebStart Flash from having duplicate host keys.

▼ To Generate the OBSDssh Package

1. **Use the cp(1) command to copy the** makeOpenSSHPackage.ksh **script to the** openssh-*x*.*xpx* **directory.**

```
$ cp makeOpenSSHPackage.ksh openssh-x.xpx
```

2. **Copy** openssh.server **to the parent directory of** openssh-*x*.*xpx*.

```
$ cp openssh.server .
```

3. Change to the `openssh-x.xpx` directory.

```
$ cd openssh-x.xpx
```

4. Edit the `makeOpenSSHPackage.ksh` **script to set the local variables for your environment.**

5. Edit `sshd_config.out` **and** `ssh_config.out` **to set up the default configuration.**

6. Use the `ksh(1)` command to make the package.

```
$ ksh ./makeOpenSSHPackage.ksh
```

7. Verify the presence of the package.

```
$ ls *pkg
OBSDssh.pkg
```

MD5 Hashes

For packages that are distributed for downloading, generate and distribute the MD5 hashes.

▼ To Generate the OpenSSH Package MD5 Hash

● **Generate the MD5 hash with the following command:**

```
$ /opt/md5/md5-sparc ./OBSDssh.pkg
MD5 (./OBSDssh.pkg) = f63c06d96dcefd919f702e234a660544
```

Solaris Security Toolkit

To facilitate the deployment of OpenSSH, the Solaris Security Toolkit software includes a `finish` script, `Finish/install-openssh.fin`, to automate the installation of the `OBSDssh` package. The `finish` script must be edited to include the version of OpenSSH, the package location, and the package name. The script will not install OpenSSH onto a Solaris 9 OE system because the Solaris Secure Shell software is provided. The script must be altered to force the installation onto a Solaris OE 9 system.

- For more information about the Solaris Security Toolkit, refer to the following Sun BluePrints publications:

  - "The Solaris™ Security Toolkit – Quick Start: *Updated for Toolkit Version 0.3*"

  - "The Solaris™ Security Toolkit – Release Notes: *Updated for Toolkit Version 0.3*"

  - "The Solaris™ Security Toolkit – Installation, Configuration, and Usage Guide: *Updated for Toolkit Version 0.3*"

  - "The Solaris™ Security Toolkit – Internals: *Updated for Toolkit Version 0.3*"

  - *Securing Systems with the Solaris Security Toolkit* by Alex Noordergraaf and Glen Brunette

---

Note – For minimized installations of the Solaris OE, the SUNWcsl package is required for OpenSSH. The SUNWzlib package is also required if the dynamic Zlib library is used to build OpenSSH.

Solaris Secure Shell Software Deployment

Deploying the Solaris Secure Shell software (Solaris 9 OE only) is simpler than deploying OpenSSH. If the end-user or larger metacluster was selected at install time, the Solaris Secure Shell software was installed as part of the operating environment. In the Solaris OE Media kit, the Solaris Secure Shell software is on CD 1 of 2.

The following example shows how to check the installed metacluster:

```
$ cat /var/sadm/system/admin/CLUSTER
CLUSTER=SUNWCall
```

Five packages comprise the Solaris Secure Shell software: SUNWsshcu, SUNWsshdr, SUNWsshdu, SUNWsshr, and SUNWsshu. For minimized JumpStart installations, the SUNWCssh cluster bundles all five together.

The following example shows how to check for the Solaris Secure Shell software packages:

```
$ pkginfo | grep ssh
system      SUNWsshcu       SSH Common, (Usr)
system      SUNWsshdr       SSH Server, (Root)
system      SUNWsshdu       SSH Server, (Usr)
system      SUNWsshr        SSH Client and utilities, (Root)
system      SUNWsshu        SSH Client and utilities, (Usr)
```

Note – For minimized installations of Solaris OE, the SUNWcsl and SUNWzlib packages are required for the Solaris Secure Shell software to function.

Custom Configuration File Distribution

Site-specific configuration files can be automatically installed by using the JumpStart software finish scripts. For more information, refer to *JumpStart Technology Effective Use in the Solaris Operating Environment*, Sun Microsystems Press, Palo Alto, 2002, by John Howard and Alex Noordergraaf.

The following code box contains an example of the finish script:

```
#!/bin/sh
# Example Secure Shell Finish script
#
echo "Copying local secure shell configuration..."
# Preserve original configuration
mv /a/etc/ssh/sshd_config /a/etc/ssh/sshd_config.orig
# Install local configuration
cp ${SI_CONFIG_DIR}/Files/sshd_config /a/etc/ssh/sshd_config
```

Solaris Fingerprint Database

The MD5 signatures for the Solaris Secure Shell software components have been integrated into the Solaris Fingerprint Database. Refer to the Sun BluePrints article "The Solaris Fingerprint Database – A Security Tool for Solaris Operating Environment Files" at:

`http://www.sun.com/blueprints/0501/Fingerprint.pdf`

For more information on the Solaris Fingerprint Database, go to:

`http://sunsolve.sun.com/pub-cgi/fileFingerprints.pl`

CHAPTER **5**

Integrating Secure Shell

Secure Shell was designed as a replacement for the Berkeley r-protocols. With the exception of key management, it can be used as a simple drop-in replacement. More advanced features that may be appropriate to your environment are also offered.

This chapter discusses integrating Secure Shell into your environment. It covers replacing rsh(1) with ssh(1) in scripts, using proxies to bridge disparate networks, limiting privileges with role-based access control (RBAC), and protecting legacy TCP-based applications. After integrating Secure Shell, insecure legacy protocols can be disabled.

Secure Shell Scripts

Automating actions with the Secure Shell client, ssh(1), is mostly a straightforward replacement of either the rsh(1) or rlogin(1) commands. There are, however, some key differences in how ssh(1) performs compared to its counterparts. Additionally, alternate authentication credentials and host keys must be addressed.

rsh(1) Versus ssh(1)

In basic usage, the ssh(1) command is a direct replacement for the rsh(1) command. The major difference between them is authentication. If an ssh(1) command is issued and a password or passphrase is needed, it will be prompted for, then the command will be executed. In this case, the rsh(1) command will fail with a *permission denied* error.

```
$ rsh host -l user cat /etc/passwd
permission denied
$ ssh host -l user cat /etc/passwd
user@host's password: password
root:x:0:1:Super-User:/:/sbin/sh
daemon:x:1:1::/:
bin:x:2:2::/usr/bin:
sys:x:3:3::/:
adm:x:4:4:Admin:/var/adm:
lp:x:71:8:Line Printer Admin:/usr/spool/lp:
uucp:x:5:5:uucp Admin:/usr/lib/uucp:
nuucp:x:9:9:uucp Admin:/var/spool/uucppublic:/usr/lib/uucp/uucico
smmsp:x:25:25:SendMail Message Submission Program:/:
listen:x:37:4:Network Admin:/usr/net/nls:
nobody:x:60001:60001:Nobody:/:
noaccess:x:60002:60002:No Access User:/:
nobody4:x:65534:65534:SunOS 4.x Nobody:/:
```

For background jobs, ssh(1) also supports the -n option to set standard input to /dev/null. Alternatively, -f sets standard input to /dev/null after password or passphrase requests, but before command execution. If no remote execution is required and only port forwarding requested, the -N option can be used (Protocol 2 only).

rcp(1) Versus scp(1)

The rcp(1) command has the same authentication problem as the rsh(1) command. As with ssh(1), the scp(1) command will prompt for passphrases and passwords as needed. Unlike the rcp(1) command, scp(1) displays a progress meter as it copies the file. This behavior can be disabled with the -q option. The scp(1) command can also optionally compress the data stream using the -C option.

The following example shows the rcp authentication problem and the scp command's progress meter.

```
$ rcp user@host:/etc/passwd /tmp
permission denied
$ scp user@host:/etc/passwd /tmp
user@host's password: password
passwd 100% |***************************|  1044        00:00
```

telnet(1) Versus ssh(1)

The telnet(1) command is occasionally used to automate connections to systems in situations in which the rlogin(1) and rsh(1) commands cannot be used. Automating a telnet(1) connection requires the script to pass the login, password, and command to the telnet(1) command to execute. The following is a Korn shell script fragment that automates the telnet(1) session:

```
(
  sleep 2
  echo login^M
  sleep 2
  echo password^M
  sleep 2
  echo command^M
  sleep 2
) | telnet hostname
```

Unlike telnet(1), this will not work with ssh(1). The Secure Shell client was programmed to ignore passwords that are passed in this manner, as shown in the following example.

```
$ ( sleep 2 ; echo "password^M"; sleep 2; ls; sleep 2 ) | ssh host -l user
Pseudo-terminal will not be allocated because stdin is not a terminal.

user@host's password: password
Permission denied, please try again.
Unable to find an authentication method
```

The ssh(1) command can be tricked around this limitation by using Expect. For more information on Expect, refer to the Expect FAQ at: http://expect.nist.gov/FAQ.html

The following is an example of a short Expect script to automate logins with passwords when using the Secure Shell:

```
#!/usr/local/bin/expect
#
#
spawn /usr/bin/ssh host -l user
expect {*password:}
send "password\r"
#
expect {*home*} exit
send "command\r"
sleep 2
#
expect {*home*} exit
```

Automated Logins

Automating logins to a system requires the script to either possess or have access to the needed authentication credentials. The problem is protecting the destination host from compromised credentials. This requires safeguarding the credentials. A balance must be struck between security and cost in terms of scalability and maintenance. There is no perfect solution.

Secure Shell provides several choices of credentials:

- Embedded passwords
- Unencrypted identities (discussed in Chapter 6)
- Embedded passphrases for encrypted user identities (discussed in Chapter 6)
- Agents

Each choice has a drawback (see TABLE 5-1). The first three choices can be defeated with read access to the secret. The fourth, agents, can be defeated with access to the machine's memory.

TABLE 5-1 Automated Login Issues

Method	Problem
Embedded passwords	Compromised by reading the script source code
Unencrypted user identities	Compromised by copying the private identity key
Embedded passphrases for encrypted user identities	Compromised by reading the script source code
Agents	Requires loading of the agent

The most resistant solution is to use agents with manually loaded keys. The problem here is twofold: maintenance and scalability. Humans are neither completely reliable nor completely dependable. The operator must be present to reload keys into the agent in the case of a failure (for example, a system crash or power loss). The operator does not scale well either. This solution requires a central machine or small cluster of machines from which remote jobs are started. A potential single-point-of-failure exists.

There is no easy, secure solution to the problem of automated remote access. A compromise solution is to use encrypted user identities in conjunction with RBAC. Secure Shell secures the network connection. The user identity limits the authorization points (the private key and passphrase must be copied first). RBAC also limits the privileges of the account.

Host Keys

The major difference in Secure Shell being a drop-in replacement for the Berkeley r-commands is host key management. Before the user can be authenticated, the destination host's Secure Shell daemon must be authenticated to the client. This is done by matching a locally stored host key copy to the host key offered by the Secure Shell daemon.

When there is no locally-stored copy, both the Solaris Secure Shell software and OpenSSH default to asking whether or not to accept the newly encountered key. This adds complexity to a script, as shown in the following example.

```
$ ssh host
The authenticity of host 'host' can't be established.
RSA key fingerprint in md5 is:
7a:71:ff:d9:6d:19:d6:d9:ef:f9:4d:3f:92:7a:77:7b
Are you sure you want to continue connecting(yes/no)?
```

The least secure method to remove this complexity is to turn off host key checking by setting StrictHostKeyChecking to no in ~/.ssh/config. The most secure solution is to acquire all of the host keys ahead of time and place them in ~/.ssh/known_hosts. See "Managing Keys and Identities" on page 71 for more information on the difficulties of key management.

Proxies

Proxies allow application-layer connections without allowing direct network connectivity. This allows applications to bridge otherwise inaccessible networks. Proxy support can be implemented in either of two ways: using alternative networking shared libraries (for instance, the runsocks command) or using the internal proxy support (ProxyCommand keyword).

The ProxyCommand interface is an external command executed with /bin/sh. The command should read from standard input and write to standard output. See ssh_config(4) and the OpenSSH source code for more details on the interface. The Solaris Secure Shell software provides support for SOCKS 5 servers through the ssh-socks5-proxy-connect(1) command and HTTP proxy servers through the ssh-http-proxy-connect(1) command. Both commands use the ProxyCommand interface and are located in the /usr/lib/ssh directory.

Note – General-usage protocols, such as HTTP and SSH, can be used to allow almost anything across the proxy, including enscapulated IP traffic. Monitor the proxy for suspicious behavior. The encrypted Secure Shell traffic hides the network content but not the endpoints or the amount of bandwidth consumed.

The following code example shows the proxy access by using the `runsocks` command. Some sites require SOCKS_SERVER and LD_LIBRARY_PATH to be explicitly set.

```
$ /usr/bin/env SOCKS_SERVER=sockserver:1080 \
LD_LIBRARY_PATH=/usr/local/socks/lib /usr/local/socks/bin/runsocks \
/opt/OBSDssh/bin/ssh remote.host.com
```

The following code example shows the proxy access by using the `ProxyCommand` interface:

```
$ ssh -o'ProxyCommand=/usr/lib/ssh/ssh-socks5-proxy-connect \
        -h socks-gw -p 1080 dmz.foo.com 22' dmz.foo.com
user@dmz's password: password
Last login: Thu Dec 10 23:03:04 2002 from foo.bar.com
Sun Microsystems Inc.   SunOS 5.8       Generic May 2001
$
```

The proxy method to access a remote host can be specified on a per-host basis with the `ProxyCommand` and `Host` keywords. The shared library method cannot be used in this manner. Note that the entire command string must be on one line.

```
Host Teach
      ProxyCommand /usr/lib/ssh/ssh-socks5-proxy-connect -h sockserver -p 1080
teach.foo.com 22
```

Role-Based Access Control

First appearing in the Solaris 8 OE release, role-based access control (RBAC) is an alternative to the all-or-nothing superuser privilege model. In the superuser (`root`) model, the power to do anything to the system—be it deleting files, adding users, starting or stopping daemons—is granted after the superuser privilege level is obtained. RBAC provides the least privilege model.

The least privilege model breaks up the capabilities of the superuser into roles. A role is a special type of user account from which privileged applications might be run. A user assumes a role with the `su(1M)` command. For example, operators might have the backup role assigned to them that allows them to run `ufsdump(1M)` with privilege. In addition, users might have one or more roles. Even `root` can be made into a role to prevent anonymous `root` logins.

In the Solaris 8 and 9 OE releases, RBAC is optional. It is not on by default because no default roles are created. For sites with earlier Solaris OE releases, an alternative to RBAC is sudo, maintained by Todd Miller. sudo provides the capabilities of su(1M) on a per-command, per-user assignment basis.

TABLE 5-2   Pros and Cons of Using RBAC, sudo, and root Shell

Name	Pro	Con
RBAC	Limits privilege by either granting limited root-level privileges or restricting what a user account can do. It is an integral feature of the Solaris OE.	Requires a change in the mindset away from the superuser model. Is not available in the Solaris 2.6 or 7 OE.
sudo	Works on non-RBAC-capable Solaris OE releases.	Must be downloaded, built, and tested. Is not Sun supported software. Grants only limited access to root-level privilege.
root Shell	Most power in using a system.	Any direct root login can do anything to the system. Console logins defeat auditing.

▼ To Use RBAC to Restrict a User to Only Copying Files

1. **Become the superuser.**

2. **Add the execution attributes of the role.**

```
# cat <<_EOM_ >> /etc/security/exec_attr
> Restricted Secure Shell:suser:cmd:::/usr/bin/scp:
> _EOM_
```

3. **Add the name of the role.**

```
# cat <<_EOM_ >> /etc/security/prof_attr
> Restricted Secure Shell:::scp access only:
> _EOM_
```

4. **Comment out** PROFS_GRANTED=Basic Solaris User **in the** /etc/security/policy.conf **file.**

5. **Assign the user the role.**

```
# cat <<_EOM_ >> /etc/user_attr
> user::::profiles=Restricted Secure Shell
> _EOM_
```

6. **Change the user's shell to a profile shell.**

```
# usermod -s /usr/bin/pfksh user
```

7. **Restart the** nscd **daemon.**

```
# /etc/init.d/nscd stop
# /etc/init.d/nscd start
```

The user will only be able to execute built-in shell commands and scp(1), as in the following example.

```
localhost$ ssh remotehost -| user
user@remotehost's password: password
Last Login: Thu Dec 12 21:51:44 2002 from someplace
remotehost$ pwd
/home/user
remotehost$ cd /
remotehost$ ls
pfksh: ls:  not found
remotehost$ pwd
/
remotehost$ cat /etc/passwd
pfksh: cat:  not found
remotehost$ exit
localhost$ ssh remotehost -| user cat /etc/passwd
Last Login: Thu Dec 12 21:51:44 2002 from someplace
pfksh: cat: not found
localhost$ scp index.html user@remotehost:index.html
user@remotehost's password: password
index.html        100% |***************************| 526 00:00
localhost$
```

For more information on RBAC, refer to the following documents:

- *Solaris 9 OE System Administration Guide*, specifically the Security Services chapter
- "Solaris Operating Environment Security: Updated for the Solaris 9 Operating Environment," December 2002, by Alex Noordergraaf and Keith Watson
- su(1M)
- roles(1)
- policy.conf(4)
- exec_attr(4)
- prof_attr(4)
- usermod(1M)
- roledel(1M)
- rolemod(1M)
- roleadd(1M)

For information on sudo, refer to: http://www.courtesan.com/sudo/

Port Forwarding

Secure Shell can enscapsulate TCP-based application data streams and then tunnel them across its secure connection to and from the client and server. This is referred to as port forwarding. Port forwarding is useful for securing communications with legacy platforms or internal systems such as the internal web site, internal Internet relay chat (IRC) network, or email access.

Port forwarding is not transparent to the application. The application requires some configuration to use the forwarded ports. For situations requiring transparency, a network-level solution such as IPsec or VPNs must be used. Port forwarding will not work for UDP-based protocols or for protocols, such as IRC DCC channels, that dynamically allocate a second data stream on a separate port.

Ports to be forwarded can either be specified on the command line or in the client configuration file (recommended for a system with multiple forwarded port). Forwarded ports can also be local (from client to server) or remote (server to the client). Port forwarding and RBAC can provide secure access to an IMAP mail server while preventing the users from having access to the server itself.

The following two examples show the local forwarding of port 8080 on the client to port 80 on the server.

This example shows forwarding using the ssh(1) command:

```
$ ssh -L8080:server:80 server
```

This example shows forwarding using the client's configuration file:

```
Host server
LocalForward 8080 server:80
```

Note – The Solaris Secure Shell software disables port forwarding by default. See "Connection and X11 Forwarding" on page 46 for more details.

▼ To Secure WebNFS Mounts With Port Forwarding

1. **Choose an unused local port and forward it to the WebNFS port on the server.**

   A different local port will be needed for each server. This connection must be maintained for the life of the mount.

   ```
   $ ssh -f -N -L3030:server:2049 server
   ```

2. **Become the superuser.**

3. **Mount the file system using the forwarded port.**

   ```
   # mount nfs://localhost:3030/export/home /mnt
   ```

Note – This procedure provides transport-level protection only for the WebNFS traffic. Using Secure Shell in this manner does not provide additional WebNFS authentication.

Insecure Service Disablement

Insecure services can be disabled by commenting them out of inetd.conf. The comment character is a hash (#). Consider making a backup copy of inetd.conf before editing. For information on inetd(1M) and inetd.conf(4), consult their respective man pages.

Remove any service not needed for your environment. In particular, remove ftp, telnet, shell, login, and exec. Consider removing echo, discard, daytime, chargen, comsat, and talk services as well. These are normally not needed.

▼ To Disable Insecure Services

1. **Become the superuser.**

2. **Edit /etc/inetd.conf and comment out insecure services.**

3. **Use the kill(2) command to send the HANGUP signal to inetd(1M).**

```
# ps -ef | grep inetd | grep -v grep
    root    153    1   0   Dec 09 ?          0:02 /usr/sbin/inetd -s
# kill -HUP 153
```

4. **Ensure that the services have been disabled.**

```
$ telnet localhost
Trying 127.0.0.1...
telnet: Unable to connect to remote host: Connection refused
$ rsh localhost
localhost: Connection refused
```

## CHAPTER 6

Managing Keys and Identities

Secure Shell uses public key cryptography to verify servers (host keys) and, optionally, users (identities) on a network that is assumed to be insecure. Challenges are made using the public key, and only the private key owner can answer the challenge correctly. The price of this security is maintaining a set of secrets (private keys) and identifiers (public keys).

The key pairs come in three forms: RSA pairs labeled RSA1 (Protocol 1 only), RSA pairs labeled RSA (Protocol 2 only), and DSA pairs labeled DSA (Protocol 2 only). The key pairs can range in size from 512 to 8192 bits. The ssh-keygen(1) command generates the key pairs.

While host and user identity key pairs are given different treatment in this book, they are essentially the same. Host keys are unencrypted user identity keys stored at a different location.

Host Keys

A host key is the public and private key pair used to authenticate the Secure Shell server to the client. The host key provides assurance that the client is communicating only with the correct host by preventing name service spoofing and man-in-the-middle attacks (that is, impersonation of the host). The Secure Shell init script generates a host key pair using the ssh-keygen(1) command if the pair is not present at startup. When the term host key is used by itself, it refers to the public key component of the pair.

At the beginning of a Secure Shell session, the server sends the public host key to the client. The client compares the key to the copy it has in its $HOME/.ssh/known_hosts file. If the key differs, the following warning message is displayed:

```
$ ssh verney
@@@@@@@@@@@@@@@@@@@@@@@@@@@@@@@@@@@@@@@@@@@@@@@@@@@@@@@@@@@@@@@@@@@@
@    WARNING: REMOTE HOST IDENTIFICATION HAS CHANGED!     @
@@@@@@@@@@@@@@@@@@@@@@@@@@@@@@@@@@@@@@@@@@@@@@@@@@@@@@@@@@@@@@@@@@@@
Someone could be eavesdropping on you right now (man-in-the-middle attack) It is also
possible that the RSA host key has been changed. The fingerprint for the RSA key sent
by the remote host is md5 88:0e:85:4c:69:e2:9d:19:c1:39:a7:b6:f8:4b:bc:d3.
Please contact your system administrator.
Add correct host key in /home/melissa/.ssh/known_hosts
Offending key is entry 7 in /home/melissa/.ssh/known_hosts
RSA host key for verney has changed and you have requested strict checking.
```

The problem is how to get the public host key securely to the client initially. The ideal solution is to use a name service for host key lookups, as in the case for IP addresses or login UIDs. This approach would eliminate the need for the client to maintain its own database of host keys. Unfortunately, Secure Shell was designed as a point-to-point solution without an integrated public key infrastructure. There has been an IETF proposal to add host key lookups to the domain name service (DNS), but neither the Solaris Secure Shell software or OpenSSH support this functionality at this time.

The simplest, but riskiest, solution is for the client to just accept a new host key when encountered. This places the client at the risk of a man-in-the-middle attack. Advise users who do this to check the host key offered by the Secure Shell server with the host key stored on the server. The two keys must match. The intermediate solution is to compare existing keys and display an error if the keys differ. If a key is newly encountered, prompt the user to accept it or abort the connection. The hardest, but safest, solution is to distribute a known_hosts file to the client with all of the host keys in it. Keys can be gathered out-of-band through the console.

In a small environment, gathering host keys out-of-band and distributing them is not a problem. For large environments, this is not the case. A program would constantly have to search for new machines and update keys as hardware is replaced or operating systems reinstalled. Then, the updated key collection would have to be distributed to every Secure Shell client. Automation can only partially alleviate this issue.

At the Solaris OE install time with the JumpStart software, the machine can be given either the current host key collection or a single server host key. Using the key provided, the system can poll for updated key collections. This approach allows the Secure Shell clients to safely acquire host key information. It does not allow Secure

Shell servers to safely register newly generated host keys. The problem is distinguishing between a host key generated from a fresh Solaris OE installation and an imposter on the network.

The obvious solution is to use `ssh-keyscan(1)` to audit the network for host keys. You will gather a list of host keys for all of the Secure Shell daemons to which your client can connect. It is a nice solution and, at face value, solves the problem of large-scale host key gathering. The catch is that you cannot trust the data because you do not know to whom you are communicating. The client could already be impersonated. You do not know if the machine actually exists. The `ssh-keyscan(1)` command can be used to audit host key changes on the network, but you will not immediately know if it is a legitimate change or an impersonation.

User Identities

A user identity is a public and private key pair used to authenticate a user to the system. Secure Shell identities provide an alternative to the standard user name and password authentication scheme. The standard scheme is by far the most popular method for authentication. However, it suffers from a number of well-documented problems. Users tend to write down their passwords, and the scheme allows dictionary attacks, social engineering, and sniffing in unsecured transmission channels. Additionally, there is nothing unique that a user can possess to distinguish that user from an imposter.

A user identity is a two-factor authentication system with three components. An identity does not suffer the majority of problems that password-based systems have. Each component must be in its proper place before the identity can be used. The first component, the public key, must be registered to the Secure Shell server. The second component, the encrypted private key (the first factor), must be possessed by the user. The third component, the passphrase to decrypt the private key (the second factor), must be known to the user.

The drawbacks of identities are increased maintenance costs and lack of scalability. If users forget their passphrases, the private keys cannot be recovered. A new identity will need to be generated and registered. On systems that allow only key-based authentication, the system administration staff will have to register identities on the users' behalf. The public key must be safely registered in a manner that cannot be tampered with in transit (for example, verifying a MD5 key fingerprint over the phone).

The identity system in OpenSSH and the Solaris Secure Shell software does not scale. The server must have file access to the public key to authenticate the identity. Every server must have its own copy of the public key, or NFS home directories must be used. Currently, there is no support to request public identity keys from some other server (for example, an LDAP server).

 Caution – With NFS home directories for which the NFS clients have write privileges, any single client can compromise the entire key-based authentication system by creating and registering identities in a user's home directory. You can reduce this risk in the Secure Shell server configurations by allowing only password authentication.

Revoking an identity can also be problematic because the work required is asymmetrical. On the user's side, the passphrase can be forgotten, and the private key can be deleted. On the server's side, the public key entry must be removed from every $HOME/.ssh/authorized_keys file. In cases in which the account is a group account and the employee is terminated, finding every entry across an enterprise can be difficult.

Identities do have their uses. They can be combined with agents (refer to "Agents" on page 75) to provide secure passphrase-free logins. They also provide a higher assurance of security than passwords.

▼ To Create an Identity

1. **Decide on the type and size of identity to create.**

2. **Create the identity and enter a passphrase.**

   The following is an example of creating a 1024-bit RSA identity:

```
$ ssh-keygen -t rsa
Enter file in which to save the key(/home/user/.ssh/id_rsa):
Generating public/private rsa key pair.
Enter passphrase(empty for no passphrase): passphrase
Enter same passphrase again: passphrase
Your identification has been saved in /home/user/.ssh/id_rsa.
Your public key has been saved in /home/user/.ssh/id_rsa.pub.
The key fingerprint is:
md5 1024 f9:42:d4:0a:af:23:26:22:14:23:4a:8c:22:14:6f:f7 user@host
```

▼ To Register an Identity

1. **Copy the public key,** *file*.pub, **to the remote Secure Shell server.**

2. **Create the** $HOME/.ssh **directory with mode** go-w **if it does not exist.**

3. **Create the** $HOME/.ssh/authorized_keys **file with mode** go-w **if it does not exist.**

4. **Add the public key to** $HOME/.ssh/authorized_keys.

▼ To Revoke an Identity

1. **On the Secure Shell server, remove the public key entry from the** $HOME/.ssh/authorized_keys **file.**

2. **On the client, remove the private key.**

Agents

A Secure Shell agent performs identity cryptographic operations on behalf of a client. Whenever a client needs to perform an operation involving a private identity key, the request is passed to the agent. The agent computes the result and passes it back to the client. The client never sees the actual key. This process requires that the agent have the key loaded. Agents allow for passphrase-free logins without the risk of unencrypted identities, as in the following example.

```
$ ssh morgan
Last login: Fri Jan 17 14:52:44 2003 from drake
Sun Microsystems Inc.    SunOS 5.9        Generic May 2002
morgan $
```

Agents work by communicating over a private UNIX socket. This socket is stored in a user-owned, mode 700 directory in the /tmp directory. The naming scheme for the socket is agent.*PID_of_the_ssh-agent*. A Secure Shell client determines agent usage by the presence of the SSH_AUTH_SOCK and SSH_AGENT_PID environment variables. If the variables are present, an attempt is made to communicate with the specified agent. If the agent does not respond or have a valid identity, the client prompts the user for authentication.

When an agent is started with the ssh-agent(1) command, Bourne shell commands are output that enable Secure Shell clients to communicate with the agent. Using the -c option, C shell commands can alternatively be output. Using the eval(1) built-in shell function, the output can be executed within the current shell by setting the needed environment variables, immediately enabling agent support to the shell and its future children.

The following is an example of starting an agent:

```
$ ssh-agent
SSH_AUTH_SOCK=/tmp/ssh-KXo27123/agent.27123; export SSH_AUTH_SOCK;
SSH_AGENT_PID=27124; export SSH_AGENT_PID;
echo Agent pid 27124;
```

The following is an example of starting an agent within the shell:

```
$ eval `ssh-agent`
Agent pid 16867
```

A newly invoked agent has no identities loaded. A separate command, ssh-add(1), controls the listing, loading, and deleting of identities. The default is to load all of the various identity types (identity for Protocol 1 only, id_dsa, and id_rsa) serially if they are present. A specific identity can be loaded by specifying it on the command line.

The following is an example of listing an empty agent:

```
$ ssh-add -l
The agent has no identities.
```

The following is an example of listing an agent with one RSA key:

```
$ ssh-add -l
md5 1024 13:cd:f7:19:87:4c:8e:5d:6c:c2:cc:51:07:af:d2:21
/home/user/.ssh/id_rsa(RSA)
```

The following is an example of adding all identities in the $HOME/.ssh file:

```
$ ssh-add
Enter passphrase for /home/user/.ssh/id_rsa: passphrase
Identity added: /home/user/.ssh/id_rsa(/home/user/.ssh/id_rsa)
Enter passphrase for /home/user/.ssh/id_dsa: passphrase
Identity added: /home/user/.ssh/id_dsa(/home/user/.ssh/id_dsa)
```

The following is an example of adding a specific identity:

```
$ ssh-add .ssh/remote
Enter passphrase for .ssh/remote: passphrase
Identity added: .ssh/remote(.ssh/remote)
```

Common Desktop Environment Support

The Common Desktop Environment (CDE) can have integrated agent support. A single agent can be started that will serve all of the child, dtterm(1) and xterm(1), terminal windows. Only one agent needs to be started for each user on the system. Agent support is added by customizing the $HOME/.dtprofile file. The changes take effect on the next session.

The ssh-add(1) command by itself cannot prompt for passphrases at the beginning of a CDE session. An X-based passphrase requestor is needed. The ssh-add(1) command can use an external passphrase requestor if the SSH_ASKPASS and DISPLAY environment variables are set. The SSH_ASKPASS variable must be set to the proper requestor $PATH. Jim Knoble has written x11-ssh-askpass, which works well for this purpose. It is available at:
http://www.jmknoble.net/software/x11-ssh-askpass/

An X-based passphrase requestor is not required to use agents with CDE. Using both the agent and the requestor, a limited form of single sign-on can be constructed. After a user is authenticated to the system for his or her CDE session and the passphrase is authenticated, that user can access any system that honors that identity without needing an additional user-visible authentication (that is, a separate password). (This is for Secure Shell logins and file transfers only.)

The following is an example of agent support for CDE in the $HOME/.dtprofile file:

```
# Start an agent for the session.
# Use Solaris Secure Shell if available; otherwise, use OpenSSH.
if [ -x /usr/bin/ssh-agent ]; then
    eval `/usr/bin/ssh-agent`
    solarisoe=1;
elif [ -x /opt/OBSDssh/bin/ssh-agent ]; then
    eval `/opt/OBSDssh/bin/ssh-agent`
    solarisoe=0;
fi
# Only add keys if x11-ssh-askpass is available.
if [ -x /usr/local/libexec/x11-ssh-askpass ]; then
    SSH_ASKPASS=/usr/local/libexec/x11-ssh-askpass ; export SSH_ASKPASS
elif [ -x /opt/OBSDssh/libexec/x11-ssh-askpass ]; then
    SSH_ASKPASS=/opt/OBSD/ssh/libexec/x11-ssh-askpass ; export SSH_ASKPASS
fi

if [ ! -z "$SSH_ASKPASS" ]; then
    if [ $solarisoe -eq 1 ]; then
        /usr/bin/ssh-add
    else
        /opt/OBSD/ssh/bin/ssh-add
    fi
fi
```

Removing Agents

When an agent is no longer needed, it should either be terminated, or the identities should be deleted from memory. If you are going to be away from the keyboard for a while, you should delete the identities. An agent is terminated by calling the ssh-agent(1) command with the -k option. Simply logging out will not terminate an agent. If a user automatically starts an agent with each login, the agents will accumulate until they are terminated with the -k option, the kill(1) command, or a system reboot.

The following is an example of unloading identities:

```
$ ssh-add -D
All identities removed.
```

The following example shows how to unset the two environment variables. Use eval(1) to cause this code to be executed within your current shell:

```
$ ssh-agent -k
unset SSH_AUTH_SOCK;
unset SSH_AGENT_PID;
echo Agent pid 16867 killed;
```

If agents were started automatically at the beginning of a CDE session, they must be terminated to prevent agent processes from building up on the system. Place the needed code in the $HOME/.dt/sessions/sessionexit file to terminate an agent at logout. See dtsession(1X) for more details.

The following is an example of the $HOME/.dt/sessions/sessionexit file:

```
#!/usr/bin/ksh
# Eliminate the agent for the session
if [ -x /usr/bin/ssh-agent ]; then
if  /usr/bin/ssh-add -D >/dev/null 2>&1; then
        eval `/usr/bin/ssh-agent -k`
fi
else if [ -x /opt/OBSDssh/bin/ssh-agent ]; then
if /opt/OBSDssh/bin/ssh-agent -D >/dev/null 2>&1; then
                eval `/opt/OBSDssh/bin/ssh-agent -k`
fi
        fi
fi
```

Agent Risks

Agents are not without their risks. The only access control to the agent socket is the private user-owned directory in the /tmp directory. Another user instance or the superuser could easily communicate with the agent and gain access to remote hosts. Additionally, the private identity keys are held in memory by the agent. Access to the memory by the superuser, a system debugger, or another instance of the same user could result in an identity compromise by reading the unencrypted private key.

The following is an example of a user agent compromise by the superuser:

```
# ls -l /tmp/ssh-gsN27129
total 0
srwxr-xr-x   1 user   staff              0 Jan 25 16:19 agent.27129
# SSH_AUTH_SOCK=/tmp/ssh-gsN27129/agent.27129; export SSH_AUTH_SOCK
# SSH_AGENT_PID=27130; export SSH_AGENT_PID
# ssh-add -l
md5 1024 bd:bc:2b:4f:5c:ee:14:b3:cd:28:e2:8b:dc:af:13:4f
/home/user/.ssh/id_rsa(RSA)
```

Agent forwarding mitigates some of the risks. With agent forwarding, the agent runs on a trusted machine, such as a personal laptop. The information needed to access the agent is passed through the Secure Shell tunnel throughout the connection chain. The intermediary Secure Shell daemons act as proxy agents. This limits the existence of the private identity key to the trusted machine. The intermediary machines need only a copy of the public identity key.

The following is an example of a simple agent forwarding session:

```
hook $ eval `/usr/bin/ssh-agent`
Agent pid 602
hook $ ssh-add
Enter passphrase for /home/user/.ssh/id_rsa: passphrase
Identity added: /home/user/.ssh/id_rsa(/home/user/.ssh/id_rsa)
hook $ cat $HOME/.ssh/config
Host *
        ForwardAgent yes
hook $ ssh blood
Last login: Mon Jan 27 21:29:10 2003 from hook
Sun Microsystems Inc.   SunOS 5.9       Generic May 2002
blood $ ssh calicojack
Last login: Mon Jan 27 21:29:41 2003 from blood
Sun Microsystems Inc.   SunOS 5.9       Generic May 2002
calicojack $ ^D
```

In this example, the user starts on hook. An agent is started, and one key is loaded. The user then logs in to blood, then to calicojack. Notice that calicojack did not prompt for authentication. The user's private key never left hook because blood was not trusted with the private identity (key).

## CHAPTER 7

Auditing

Auditing and logging provide a historical record of what happened on the system. Auditing can provide accountability by tracing the actions of a user or process. It can state what commands were executed, what files were opened, and when the actions occurred. Logging provides a record of what a daemon did. This record can include basic logging information, such as when a connection was served, or include detailed diagnostic information for debugging. Remember that audit trails and logs are useless if they are never reviewed.

Auditing Overview and Basic Procedures

The SunSHIELD Basic Security Module (BSM) provides auditing capabilities at a granular level. This capability was added to meet the C2 level of the Trusted Computer System Evaluation Criteria (TCSEC). TCSEC has been superseded by the Common Criteria. The Solaris OE has been evaluated at Evaluation Assurance Level (EAL) 4 under the Controlled Access Protection Profile (CAPP). It is possible to audit events on a system-wide basis, for a particular user, or for combination of both.

The auditing tradeoff is to minimize performance degradation while auditing events. It is not cost effective to audit all events. The performance loss and disk space costs are too high. Audit only selected events that generate meaningful information. For example, audit command executions for a user account that should only be opening files.

Note – By default, BSM is disabled in the Solaris OE.

BSM works by enabling a third user ID, the audit ID. This ID is set at login time and inherited by all child processes. Unlike the real and effective user IDs, the audit ID does not change when running a setuid(2) program. The audit ID is recorded in the audit trail with each audited event. All of the actions a user performs throughout the session are tied to this ID, regardless of which su(1M) or setuid(2) events occur. See getuid(2) and getauid(2) for more information about user IDs.

The auditing daemon, auditd(1M), controls the creation and location of the audit trails (that is, the files containing the auditing information). auditd(1M) reads the audit_control(4), audit_class(4), and audit_user(4) files to determine which trails to audit (audit_control(4) and audit_user(4) files) and where to write the trails (audit_control(4)). The default is to log only the login and logout events of the root user. The default audit trail location is /var/audit. See audit(1M), auditd(1M), audit_control(4), audit_class(4), and audit_user(4) for more information.

Unlike the majority of system logs, audit trails are stored in a binary format. The praudit(1M) command converts the audit trails to an ASCII format that can be read or otherwise processed. For large audit trails, the auditreduce(1M) command can be used to select only the events of interest. See auditreduce(1M), praudit(1M), and audit.log(4) for more information.

Only a cursory introduction to BSM has been presented. For more information, consult the sections on BSM auditing in *System Administration Guide: Security Services* available at docs.sun.com, the "Auditing in the Solaris 8 Operating Environment," Sun BluePrints OnLine article, by Osser and Noordergraaf, audit(1M), auditd(1M), auditreduce(1M), bsmconv(1M), and praudit(1M).

▼ To Configure Auditing to Audit a Systemwide Event

In this procedure, all login and logout events are audited.

1. **Become the superuser.**

2. **Edit /etc/security/audit_control by changing the following:**

```
flags:
```

to

```
flags:lo
```

▼ To Configure Auditing to Audit Commands Run by a Particular User

1. **Become the superuser.**

2. **Edit** `/etc/security/audit_user` **by appending the following:**

```
userlogin:ex:no
```

▼ To Enable Auditing

1. **Become the superuser.**

2. **Put the system into system administrator mode.**

```
# /usr/sbin/init 1
```

3. **Enable the BSM.**

```
# /etc/security/bsmconv
This script is used to enable the Basic Security Module (BSM).
Shall we continue with the conversion now? [y/n] y
bsmconv: INFO: checking startup file.
bsmconv: INFO: move aside /etc/rc3.d/S81volmgt.
bsmconv: INFO: turning on audit module.
bsmconv: INFO: initializing device allocation files.

The Basic Security Module is ready.
If there were any errors, please fix them now.
Configure BSM by editing files located in /etc/security.
Reboot this system now to come up with BSM enabled.
```

Caution – The bsmconv(1M) command inserts set abort_enable = 0 in system(4). This disables stopping a system with the Stop-A key sequence or by sending a break over a serial line. If this is not desired, remove this line from /etc/system before rebooting.

4. **Reboot the system.**

```
# reboot
```

5. **Log in and verify that auditing has started by ensuring the presence of the log file.**

The log file should be present and have the string not_terminated after the starting date.

```
# ls -l /var/audit
-rw-------   1 root        root        79331 Jan 20 15:29
20030120232604.not_terminated.bounty
```

▼ To Audit the System

1. **Become the superuser.**

2. **Display the system audit events with** praudit *audit_trail*.

```
# praudit /var/audit/20030120232604.not_terminated.bounty
```

▼ To Audit a User

1. **Become the superuser.**

2. **Display the audit events for the user.**

```
# auditreduce -u user | praudit
```

In the case of a large number of events, only particular class events can be listed (for example, only login or logout events).

```
# auditreduce -u root -c lo | praudit
file,Mon Jan 20 15:28:55 2003, + 0 msec,
header,81,2,login - local,,Mon Jan 20 15:28:55 2003, + 83 msec
subject,root,root,other,root,other,324,324,0 0 bounty
text,successful login
return,success,0
header,81,2,login - local,,Mon Jan 20 16:10:42 2003, + 651 msec
subject,root,root,other,root,other,321,321,0 0 bounty
text,successful login
return,success,0
file,Mon Jan 20 16:10:42 2003, + 0 msec,
```

▼ To Disable Auditing

If auditing is no longer needed, the following procedure will disable it.

1. **Become the superuser.**

2. **Put the system into system administrator mode.**

```
# /usr/sbin/init 1
```

3. **Disable the BSM.**

```
# /etc/security/bsmunconv
```

4. **Reboot the system.**

```
# reboot
```

5. Log in and verify that the auditing has stopped.

The last log file has a termination date.

```
# ls -l /var/audit
total 186
-rw-------   1 root      root       79343 Jan 20 15:49
20030120232604.20030120234907.bounty
-rw-------   1 root      root       14465 Jan 20 16:25
20030120235034.20030121002529.bounty
```

OpenSSH

Any program that provides entry into the system needs to incorporate the BSM auditing hooks. OpenSSH does not have the needed support. (This was true as of OpenSSH 3.5p1. Support may be added in a future version. The OpenSSH portability team has been provided the necessary code.)

Two problems with OpenSSH connections occur after BSM is enabled. First, no actions by users who enter the system are audited. Second, the user's audit characteristics are not properly set up. The Solaris Secure Shell software has full integration with BSM. It does not have the problems of OpenSSH.

Note – Do not attempt to use BSM auditing in conjunction with privilege separation. The two are not compatible.

cron(1M)

The problem with BSM auditing is often discovered when cron(1M) stops working. The problem is that the user's cron audit file (that is, /var/spool/cron/crontabs/root.au) has become corrupted. The corruption occurs whenever the crontab is changed through an OpenSSH connection with improperly set audit characteristics.

The following is a fragment of the /var/cron/log file.

```
! cron audit problem. job failed (/usr/bin/true) for user root
Mon Jan 20 19:55:00 2003
```

There are three workarounds to this problem. Each has a significant negative consequence. First, disable BSM auditing. No corruption will occur, but neither will there be an audit trail for accountability. Second, set UseLogin to yes in sshd_config(4), then restart the Secure Shell daemon. This eliminates both port and X forwarding, which your users may have come to expect, and it is not always effective because non-interactive sessions may still cause corruption. Third, after connecting through OpenSSH, execute telnet(1) or rlogin(1) by using the loopback interface. Auditing characteristics will be correctly set on the second login.

Patching

If the workarounds are insufficient, the only recourse is to patch the OpenSSH source before building it. Darren Moffat originally provided a patch for version 3.1p1. John Jackson has been periodically updating the patch as new OpenSSH versions appear. (As of this writing, he produced updated patches for versions 3.4p1 and 3.5p1.) The updated patches and instructions can be retrieved from Bug 125 in the Portable OpenSSH bug tracking database at: http://bugzilla.mindrot.org/show_bug.cgi?id=125

For more information on the BSM and OpenSSH interactions, refer to Bugs 2 and 125 in the Portable OpenSSH bug tracking database.

Logging

The standard facility for logging on the Solaris OE is syslog(3C). Both the Solaris Secure Shell software and OpenSSH, along with the majority of the system daemons, make use of this. The syslog facility works by having the program transmit syslog messages to the syslog daemon, syslogd(1M). A syslog message consists of a header and a body. The header consists of a tag string (usually the process name), a facility code, a severity code, a timestamp, and, often, the process ID. The message body is the information to be logged.

The following is an example of Secure Shell daemon log file messages:

```
Jan 20 22:19:29 bounty sshd[489]: [ID 800047 auth.info] Accepted
password for pablo from 192.168.0.10 port 48388 ssh2
Jan 20 22:19:59 bounty sshd[499]: [ID 800047 auth.info] Accepted
publickey for max from 192.168.0.15 port 48389 ssh2
```

> **Note –** OpenSSH logging is not affected by the status of BSM.

The syslogd(1M) daemon processes messages based on their facility and severity codes. The facility code denotes what part of the system the message came from (that is, kern for the kernel, mail for the mailing system—procmail, sendmail, or IMAP, or auth for the authorization system—login or su). The severity code lists the priority of the message (that is, emerg for emergency, err for error, or INFO for informational. This code pair is written as facility.severity (for example, kern.debug or mail.err). How the daemon processes the messages, whether it is to write them to the console, a file, or transmit over the network to a central logging host, is determined by the configuration in syslog.conf(4).

Both the Solaris Secure Shell software and OpenSSH default to facility and severity codes of auth.info. The facility and severity codes can be changed with the SyslogFacility keyword. The default syslogd(1M) configuration is to drop auth.info messages. This creates the impression that neither the Solaris Secure Shell software nor OpenSSH is producing any logging information. The syslogd(1M) configuration must be changed to retain the logging information.

▼ To Enable Secure Shell Logging

1. **Become the superuser.**

2. **Edit** syslog.conf**(4) by adding the following:**

```
auth.info      /var/adm/sshd.log
```

A tab must separate the two fields.

> **Note –** This log file will accumulate everything at the auth.info facility and severity code level, including non-Secure Shell daemon messages.

3. **Create the log file.**

```
# touch /var/adm/sshd.log
# chmod 600 /var/adm/sshd.log
```

4. **Signal** `syslogd`**(1M) to reread** `syslog.conf`**(4).**

```
# pkill -HUP syslogd
```

The output level of logging information (verbosity) is controlled by the `LogLevel` keyword. The default level, `INFO`, is basic information, such as how (password or key-based), when, and from where, a user authenticated to the system. The example messages shown above are from the default logging level. The highest verbosity is debug. The Secure Shell daemon will log every step that it takes from binding to a port, through handling connections, and, finally, to terminating on the `DEBUG` level. This level can produce a significant data stream on a system with many Secure Shell connections. It should only be used to diagnose system problems. Debugging messages are output at the `auth.debug` level. You can direct them to a separate log file.

For more information, refer to `syslog`(3C), `syslogd`(1M), and `syslog.conf`(4). Additional information can be found in *System Administration Guide: Advanced Administration* available on `docs.sun.com`.

## CHAPTER 8

Measuring Performance

Secure Shell has greater resource usage than its insecure counterparts. It consumes more processor time and bandwidth than a corresponding Berkeley r-protocol connection. For a limited number of connections, such as a single-system administrator connection, the additional resource consumption is not an issue. Performance can become a problem, however, when a large number of connections must be sustained.

The performance measurements presented here are relative to the equipment and software used to generate them. See "Performance Test Methodology" on page 155 for the details. In delivering Secure Shell as part of a solution, do your own performance testing if you have questions. The results will vary depending on the platform used, the processor speed, the Solaris OE release, and other factors.

For performance measurements beyond what vmstat(1M), iostat(1M), sar(1), time(1), ps(1), and snoop(1M) provide, refer to the SE Toolkit by Adrian Cockcroft and Rich Pettit. The SE Toolkit is not a Sun Microsystems-supported product. It is available at: http://www.setoolkit.com/

Note – For this chapter, consider any measurements to be rough estimates. Do not depend on these numbers. Do your own performance analysis if performance goals must be met.

Bandwidth Performance

Secure Shell replaces both interactive and file transfer protocols. Each has different bandwidth consumption characteristics. Interactive protocols, such as rlogin(1) and ssh(1), are intermittent (bursty) in their bandwidth usage, with the pauses occurring when the commands are executed or when the user reacts to the output. File transfer protocols, such as ftp(1) or scp(1), have sustained bandwidth usage.

Interactive Sessions

For interactive sessions, Secure Shell bandwidth consumption is on par with its insecure counterparts. The only significant difference is the additional processor time needed for the encryption and integrity checks. This difference is difficult to notice on high-latency network links.

telnet	Packet count	99
	Bytes transferred	8952
rlogin	Packet count	69
	Bytes transferred	6320
ssh	Packet count	63
	Bytes transferred	8712

FIGURE 8-1   Interactive Session Performance for `ls /`

telnet	Packet count	326
	Bytes transferred	225096
rlogin	Packet count	380
	Bytes transferred	262318
ssh	Packet count	313
	Bytes transferred	264272

FIGURE 8-2   Interactive Session Performance for `cat /usr/dict/words`

File Transfers

For small file transfers, Secure Shell bandwidth consumption, using scp(1) for file transfers, is on par with ftp(1). For large file transfers, Secure Shell consumes significantly more bandwidth. Interactive sessions that produce large amounts of data could also exhibit this behavior (for example, port forwarding of WebNFS mounts).

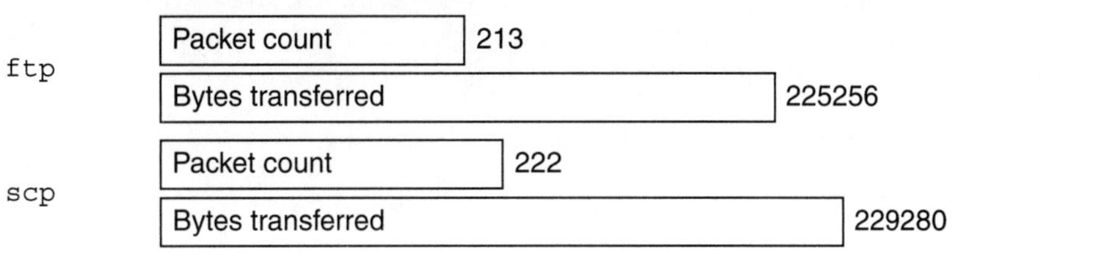

FIGURE 8-3 File Transfer Performance for `/usr/dict/words`

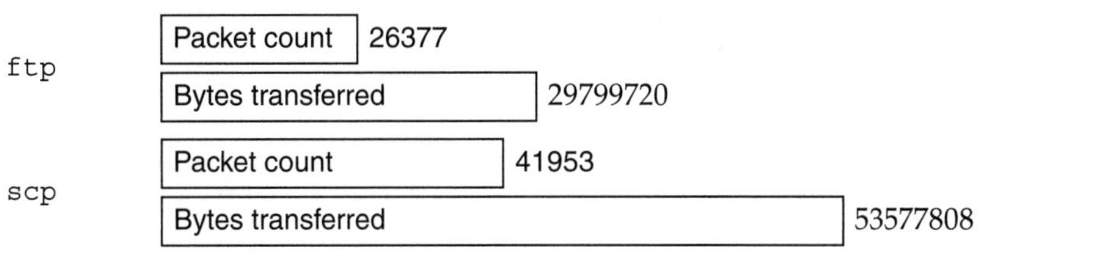

FIGURE 8-4 File Transfer Performance for the Solaris 8 2/02 OE SPARC Install Image

Symmetric Cipher Performance

Clients have a choice of ciphers for their bulk encryption work. In bulk encryption, the majority of processor cycles are consumed in the Secure Shell protocol. For sessions transferring large amounts of data, such as file transfers, the choice of cipher can have a large impact on overall performance. The three ciphers shown in the following graph are Advanced Encryption Standard (AES), Blowfish, and 3DES. These ciphers are common to both the Solaris Secure Shell software and OpenSSH.

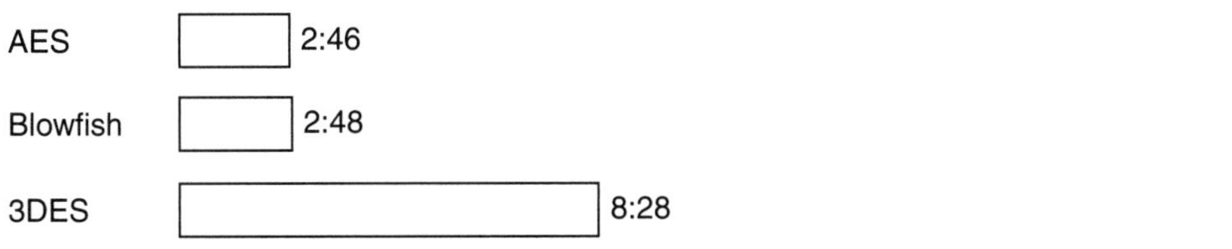

FIGURE 8-5 Time to Transfer a 678-Mbyte File (in minutes:seconds)

The preceding graph shows that Blowfish and AES have similar levels of performance. Some sites might prefer Blowfish over AES because AES has no long-term history of cryptanalytic work and because it is a United States government-supported algorithm.

3DES is an algorithm designed to be implemented in hardware. The poor performance of a software implementation means that this algorithm should be used only in regulatory environments that require it or to support legacy systems that do not support Blowfish or AES.

Identity Generation

Identity key costs are asymmetrical. They are very cheap to produce, but very expensive to break. It takes longer to type the command to generate a 512-bit RSA identity than it does to generate the identity. In late 1999, the factorization of RSA-155 (512-bit) was accomplished at the estimated cost of 8000 MIPS per year. It is believed that 1024-bit keys are infeasible to break (at least until the advent of large-scale, effective quantum computers).

Note – Because 512-bit identities can be compromised, do not use them. Use 1024-bit or larger identities.

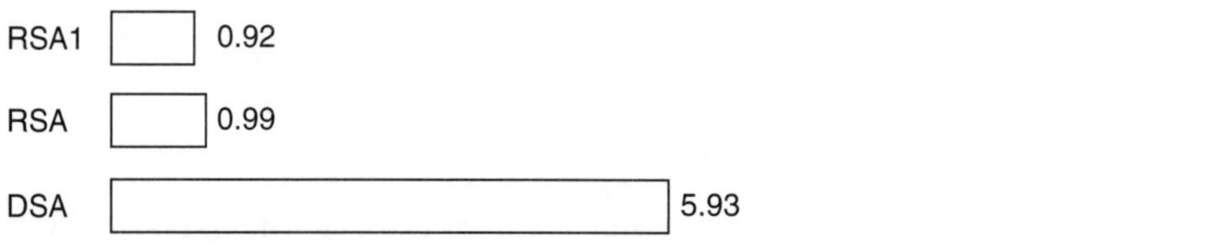

RSA1 ☐ 0.92

RSA ☐ 0.99

DSA ☐ 5.93

FIGURE 8-6 Generation Times for 1024-bit Identities (in seconds)

The costs of generating an identity key are mostly processing time, plus some entropy, and a small amount of disk space. In terms of performance, generating a single key is not a problem. A second or two of real-time for computing the key will not be a difficulty. The problem comes with generating very large keys or generating a large number of keys.

The Solaris Secure Shell software supports identities up to 8192 bits. Given that a 4096-bit DSA identity can take upwards of 20 minutes to generate and that key generation times grow exponentially with the linear increase in key size, it is not practical to generate a key that large. (During the performance tests, the attempt was abandoned after several days of processing time.)

For an application requiring a large number of identities, such as a one-time use identity system or a mass deployment of Secure Shell, the cost of generating a thousand keys can become an issue. As the following charts show, processing time is not much of a concern. One item to be aware of is entropy exhaustion. If your entropy source is exhausted, weaker identities will be generated.

In general, RSA Protocol 1 and RSA Protocol 2 identities take roughly the same amount of time to generate. DSA identities are considerably more expensive to generate. Both DSA and RSA are considered secure at key sizes of 1024 bits. The decision of which to use should be based on preference, performance, and regulatory requirements.

Key Size	Time
512 bits	0.17
1024 bits	0.92
1536 bits	2.86
2048 bits	5.21
2560 bits	15.74
3072 bits	31.06
3584 bits	50.11
4096 bits	102.31

FIGURE 8-7 Generation Times for RSA Protocol 1 (RSA1) Identities (in seconds)

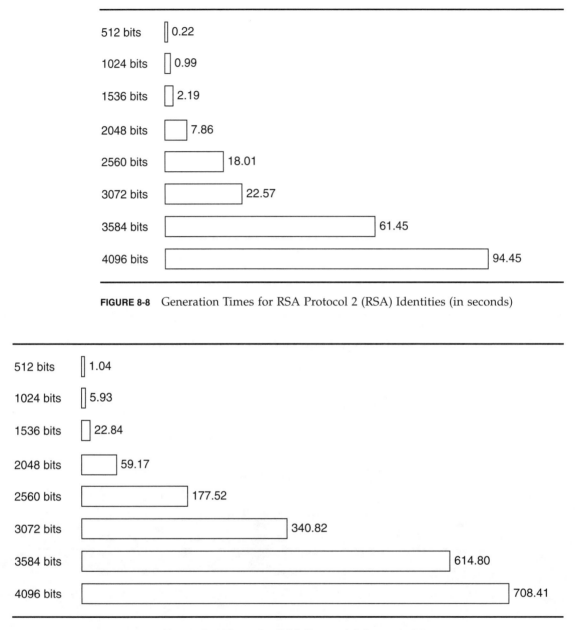

FIGURE 8-8 Generation Times for RSA Protocol 2 (RSA) Identities (in seconds)

FIGURE 8-9 Generation Times for DSA Protocol 2 (in seconds)

Performance Problems

Performance troubles appear most often in the form of slow startup or slow connections. Slow startups are usually the result of either entropy source problems or name service problems.

Slow Connections

Slow or intermittent connections are more likely a symptom of network problems, such as high latency or lack of server resources, than a problem with Secure Shell (the exception is the use of 3DES as the symmetric cipher). This will cause relatively slow performance for file transfers, as shown in the following example:

```
Jan  5 14:20:08 keelhaul genunix: WARNING: hme0: No response
from Ethernet network : Link down -- cable problem?
Jan  5 14:20:52 keelhaul genunix: NOTICE: hme0: fault cleared
in device; service available
Jan  5 14:20:52 keelhaul genunix: NOTICE: hme0: Internal
Transceiver Selected.
```

Slow Client Startup

Slow client startup could be the symptom of a number of problems, such as slow entropy source, a large number of host key entries in ~/.ssh/known_hosts, large identities (greater than 1024 bits), name service issues such as DNS or NIS host look-ups, or network difficulties. The first item to check is the name service, followed by the network itself. Use the debug command-line option and console messages to diagnose problems, as in the following example of a truss(1) fragment of an ssh(1) session:

```
[...]
stat("/usr/lib/libnsl.so.1", 0xFFBFED24)          = 0
munmap(0xFF340000, 8192)                           = 0
open("/etc/services", O_RDONLY)                    = 4
fstat64(4, 0xFFBFF388)                             = 0
brk(0x000EFA18)                                    = 0
brk(0x000F1A18)                                    = 0
fstat64(4, 0xFFBFF230)                             = 0
ioctl(4, TCGETA, 0xFFBFF314)                       Err#25 ENOTTY
read(4, " # i d e n t\t " @ ( # )".., 8192)        = 3869
llseek(4, 0xFFFFFFFFFFFFF299, SEEK_CUR)            = 438
close(4)                                           = 0
door_info(3, 0xFFBFD388)                           = 0
door_call(3, 0xFFBFD370)                           = 0
door_info(3, 0xFFBFD308)                           = 0
door_call(3, 0xFFBFD2F0)           (sleeping...)
```

The truss(1) command is a very useful problem-solving tool. It shows what system calls are being executed, whether they succeed or fail, and if they are hanging (that is, sleeping). The preceding code fragment shows that ssh(1) is hanging in door_call(3DOOR). The problem was that the network cable had come loose.

Slow Server Startup

The first time a server is started, host keys must be generated. This takes some time, normally several seconds. Slow machines or machines with limited entropy could cause the process to take a minute or more. Slow successive startups signify a slow entropy source or problems reading necessary files (that is, NFS timeouts or slow name service). Use the debug command-line options, configuration options, or the truss(1) command to diagnose the problem.

Sizing

As the bandwidth numbers showed, replacing telnet(1) with Secure Shell for interactive connections should have no discernible performance impact. The impact can be measurable, but it is doubtful that a user at the keyboard will be able to tell the difference. This replacement should scale well in environments in which the connection method, such as administrative connections, is secondary to the work being done. It will break down for large numbers of users as the extra processor requirements become a factor. Adding additional processor resources could be required. You can mitigate the problem by tuning Secure Shell to not use the 3DES algorithm.

For large file transfers, particularly to multiple hosts, the replacement of FTP with SCP can have serious performance impacts. The additional bandwidth requirement can easily reduce the number of possible hosts that can be served. Also, each file transfer is a separate encrypted session. With interactive sessions, there are plenty of pauses (between keystrokes or examination of the command output) to grab spare processor cycles. For file transfers, there is a sustained processor load. Replacing an anonymous FTP server with Secure Shell is not advisable.

One alternative would be to encrypt the data using GNU Privacy Guard, transfer the data by FTP, then use SCP to transfer the decryption key, assuming the data needs to be secret. If the data is not sensitive, distributing signed hashes should provide good enough protection. An alternative would be to use a commercial multicast solution that supports encryption to transfer the data.

For information on sizing, consult the publications by Adrian Cockcroft and Brian Wong listed in the "Bibliography" on page 185.

## CHAPTER 9

Examining Case Studies

Secure Shell can be used for more than just protecting a remote login. For instance, it can be used to solve actual problems. This chapter includes solutions such as building a simple point-to-point virtual private network and linking two disparate networks through an intermediary bastion host.

The examples shown here use the Solaris Secure Shell software and the Solaris PPP 4.0 software in the Solaris 9 12/02 OE release. The examples could be done with OpenSSH and the ASPP software from earlier Solaris OE releases. The latter form is not presented here. For more information on the Solaris PPP 4.0 software, consult pppd(1M) and the *Solaris 9 System Administration: Resource Management and Network Services* book. This book is part of the Solaris 9 System Administration collection available on docs.sun.com.

A Simple Virtual Private Network

Using Secure Shell and the point-to-point protocol (PPP), a simple encrypted point-to-point link can be created between any two accessible hosts. This can be useful in situations where IPsec is not available, as in the case of hosts that require proxies for mutual communication. In the case of direct network-accessible hosts, the inconvenience of having to forward ports is avoided.

In the following example, a simple point-to-point link is created. The originating host uses 192.168.0.34 as the PPP interface's bound IP address. The destination host uses 192.168.0.35. Both hosts are set up with no additional authentication for PPP. This allows any user account to initiate the PPP link.

▼ To Set Up the Destination Side

1. Become the superuser.

2. Create the `/etc/ppp/options` **file with the following contents:**

```
lock
nodefaultroute
noauth
notty
192.168.0.35:192.168.0.34
```

▼ To Set Up the Originating Side

1. Become the superuser.

2. Create the `/etc/ppp/options` **file with the following contents:**

```
noauth
192.168.0.34:192.168.0.35
```

▼ To Initiate the Link

1. Execute the pppd(1M) **command from the originating side.**

```
$ pppd pty "ssh host -l user /usr/bin/pppd" updetach
Using interface sppp0
Connect: sppp0 <--> /dev/pts/2
user@host's password: password
Peer Identification: ppp-2.4.0b1 (Sun Microsystems, Inc., Sep  6 2002 09:57:20)
local  IP address 192.168.0.34
remote IP address 192.168.0.35
```

2. Verify the link.

```
$ ifconfig sppp0
sppp0: flags=10008d1<UP,POINTOPOINT,RUNNING,NOARP,MULTICAST,IPv4>mtu 1500 index 8
        inet 192.168.0.34 --> 192.168.0.35 netmask ffffff00

$ ping 192.168.0.35
192.168.0.35 is alive
```

Linking Networks Through a Bastion Host

Using both local and remote forwarding, a Secure Shell session can be set up between any two hosts, provided that there is an intermediary to go through. The intermediary could be one host or a series of hosts and could involve proxies. PPP could be used to provide direct IP connectivity. Having a session between the two endpoints prevents the intermediary from examining the traffic.

This example has three hosts: calicojack, bastion, and bellamy. Neither calicojack nor bellamy can see each other. They both can see bastion. The user on bellamy wants to log in to calicojack. The following diagram shows the relationships between these hosts.

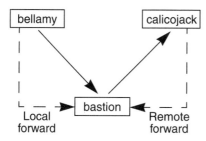

FIGURE 9-1 Linking Networks Example

▼ To Set Up the Destination Side

● **Start the reverse forward.**

```
calicojack $ ssh -f -N -R3030:localhost:22 bastion
```

▼ To Set Up the Originating Side

1. **Start the local forward.**

```
bellamy $ ssh -L3030:localhost:3030 bastion
```

2. **Connect through the two forwards.**

```
bellamy $ ssh -p 3030 localhost
user@localhost's password: password
Last login: Wed Jan 15 13:53:09 2003 from localhost
Sun Microsystems Inc.    SunOS 5.9       Generic May 2002
calicojack /home/user $
```

## CHAPTER 10

Resolving Problems and Finding Solutions

This chapter discusses some of the problems most frequently encountered when using Secure Shell and how to report those problems. It also contains information about patches and solutions for commonly asked questions.

Problems

This section contains descriptions of and solutions to the problems most frequently encountered when using Secure Shell.

Server Does Not Produce Log File Output

By default, sshd produces auth.info-level messages. The default configuration of syslogd(1M) ignores these. syslog.conf(4) must have an entry added for these messages. Then, the log file needs to be created, and syslogd needs a HUP signal, as in the following example.

```
# grep auth.info /etc/syslog.conf
auth.info       /var/adm/sshd.log
# touch /var/adm/sshd.log
# pkill -HUP syslogd
```

Note – A tab must separate the two fields.

If debugging information is needed, add an entry for `auth.debug`.

Public Key Authentication Is Not Working

Verify that the public key is in the remote `~/.ssh/authorized_keys` file and that the file is neither group nor world writable. See "Debugging a Secure Shell Connection" on page 110 for more information.

Trusted Host Authentication Is Not Working

Verify that this feature has not been disabled in the `sshd_config` file and that `ssh(1)` is installed as `setuid root`.

X Forwarding Is Not Working

Verify the following:

- `X11Forwarding` has been set to `yes` in the `sshd_config` file on the destination server.
- X forwarding has been enabled on the client by `ForwardX11` being set to `yes` in the `ssh_config` file or by `ssh(1)` being executed with the `-X` option.
- `UseLogin` has been set to `no`.
- The `$DISPLAY` environment variable has been set correctly.

Wildcards and Shell Variables Fail on the scp(1) Command Line

Wildcards and shell variables must be escaped, or the local shell will expand them, as in the following example:

```
$ scp panther@mainwaring:${HOME}/public_html/ssh.html /tmp/toast
panther@mainwaring's password: password
scp: /home/panther/public_html/ssh.html: No such file or directory
$ scp panther@mainwaring:\$\{HOME\}/public_html/ssh.html /tmp/toast
panther@mainwaring's password: password
ssh.html                100% |****************************|  3529        00:00
```

Superuser (root) Is Unable to Log In

To permit superuser logins, the PermitRootLogin keyword must be set to yes in the sshd_config file.

Note – If root is a role in the role-based access control model, then the value of PermitRootLogin is overridden by pam_roles(5).

Startup Performance Is Slow

Verify that ssh(1) is using /dev/urandom by using truss to check that /dev/urandom is opened successfully, as in the following example.

```
$ truss -t open -o /tmp/ssh.trace ssh localhost
<either login then logout or let the connection timeout>
$ grep random /tmp/ssh.trace
open64("/dev/urandom", O_RDONLY)                = 5
open("/dev/urandom", O_RDONLY)                  = 6
```

Protocol 1 Clients Are Unable to Connect to Solaris Secure Shell Systems

By default, the Solaris Secure Shell software disables Protocol 1. Comment out the Protocol 2 line with a hash (#) symbol. Uncomment the Protocol 2,1 line. Restart the sshd(1M) daemon by sending the HUP signal.

The following example shows the Solaris Secure Shell defaults:

```
# Only v2 (recommended)
Protocol 2
```

The following example shows how to enable Protocol 1:

```
# Only v2 (recommended)
# Protocol 2
#
# Both v1 and v2 (not recommended)
Protocol 2,1
```

Privilege Separation Does Not Work in the Solaris Secure Shell Software

This functionality does not currently exist.

cron(1M) Is Broken

OpenSSH lacks integration into BSM by not correctly assigning an audit ID. This causes both BSM and cron(1M) to fail when a crontab entry is edited. A workaround for crontab editing is to use Telnet to connect to the local host through the loopback interface. Telnet will invoke login(1), which sets the audit ID correctly. The Solaris Secure Shell software does not have this problem.

Message-of-the-Day Is Displayed Twice

By default, `PrintMotd` is set to `yes` in the `sshd_config` file. In the Solaris OE, the login shell is expected to display the message-of-the-day. The Secure Shell daemon should not display it. Set `PrintMotd` to `no` to stop this behavior.

Problem Reports

This section contains information on how to report a problem with the Secure Shell software.

OpenSSH

First, check the OpenSSH mailing lists in "Resources" on page 181 to see if the problem has already been found and a solution presented. Second, go to `http://www.openssh.com/report.html` for information on problem reporting. This site is used for reporting a problem with the software (that is, a bug). It is not used for user support.

Solaris Secure Shell Software

For customers with a support contract, a problem with the Solaris Secure Shell software can be reported through technical support at 1-800-USA-4SUN.

Patches

This section contains information about finding patches for the Secure Shell environment.

OpenSSH

The OpenSSH portability team does not release patches. Instead, updated versions of OpenSSH are released. If you are responding to a vulnerability or desiring a new feature, build the latest version, and test it for suitability to your environment.

Solaris Secure Shell Software

Patches are located at the SunSolve℠ program web site (http://sunsolve.Sun.com/). At time this writing, only Patch ID 113273 for the Solaris 9 OE SPARC release exists.

Solutions

This section contains solutions for commonly asked questions about Secure Shell.

Debugging a Secure Shell Connection

When sessions are encrypted, debugging tools such as tcpdump(1M) and truss(1) provide less assistance. On the client, debug information is generated with the -v flag. Up to three -v flags can be used to increase the debugging information verbosity. The flag for the server is -d. Alternatively, the level of debugging information can be set using the LogLevel keyword in the configuration file (~/.ssh/config for the client and sshd_config for the server).

The following example shows debugging on the command line:

```
$ ssh -v -v -v bonnet
```

The following example shows how to set up debugging by using the ~/.ssh/config or sshd_config file:

```
LogLevel DEBUG
```

Understanding Differences in OpenSSH and Solaris Secure Shell Software

The Solaris Secure Shell software has BSM support, proxy commands (ssh-socks5-proxy-connect and ssh-http-proxy-connect), localization and internationalization support, and configurable login attempts (MaxAuthTries and MaxAuthTriesLog). OpenSSH does not support these features. OpenSSH supports privilege separation and additional ciphers that Solaris Secure Shell software does not support.

Integrating Solaris Secure Shell and SEAM (Kerberos)

Presently, there is no integration between the Solaris Secure Shell software and SEAM.

Forcing Remote X11 Users to Use Secure Shell Sessions

For Solaris 9 OE systems, add -nolisten tcp to Xsun in /usr/dt/config/Xservers, then restart the X daemon. Make sure to preserve a copy of Xservers to maintain changes in case of patches or OS upgrades.

Determining the Server Version String

When clients connect, the server identifies itself with a version string. Connecting by Telnet to the server and sending a carriage return will return the version string and close the connection, as in the following example.

```
$ (sleep 1; print "\n") |telnet localhost 22
Trying 127.0.0.1...
Connected to localhost.
Escape character is '^]'.
SSH-2.0-Sun_SSH_1.0
Connection to localhost closed by foreign host.
```

Altering the Server Version String

In OpenSSH, the version string can be altered by editing the value of `SSH_VERSION` in `version.h` before compilation. Changing the version string to obscure the specific OpenSSH release risks breaking clients that use the version string to work around server bugs. The version string cannot be changed in the Solaris Secure Shell software.

CERT Advisory CA-2002-18

The default configuration of the Solaris Secure Shell software is not believed to be vulnerable. To be vulnerable, `sshd_config` must be updated to contain the following:

```
PAMAuthenticationViaKBDInt yes
KbdInteractiveAuthentication yes
```

The default for `KbdInteractiveAuthentication` is no. Patch ID 113273 fixes this problem.

Secure Shell Usage

This appendix is a basic guide to Secure Shell usage. For more information, refer to the *Solaris 9 System Administration Guide: Security Services* book at docs.sun.com and the following man pages:

- scp(1)
- sftp(1)
- sftp-server(1M)
- ssh(1)
- sshd(1M)
- ssh-add(1)
- ssh-agent(1)
- ssh-keygen(1)
- ssh_config(4)
- sshd_config(4)

Client Usage

This section covers the client-side usage of Secure Shell. The basics of remote host connections and job executions, along with file transfers, are covered. The more advanced client usage of identities, agents, port and X forwarding, and proxies are also covered. Examples are used to demonstrate the various features. This is meant to be a brief introduction, not an in-depth guide.

Connecting to a Host

The following example shows the basic syntax of the ssh(1) command:

```
$ ssh remote
user@remote's password: password
Last login: Wed Dec 18 00:12:38 2002 from someplace
Sun Microsystems Inc.   SunOS 5.9       Generic May 2002
remote $
```

Executing a Command on a Remote Host

The ssh(1) command's remote job form is ssh *remote_host job*, as shown in the following example:

Note – Shell variables are expanded on the local side, unless they are escaped.

```
$ ssh remote cat /var/sadm/system/admin/CLUSTER
user@remote's password: password
CLUSTER=SUNWCXall
```

Copying a File

The scp(1) command's form is scp *source destination*. The following example demonstrates how to copy a local file to a remote host:

```
$ scp 816-5241.pdf remote:/tmp
user@remote's password: password
816-5241.pdf          100% |***************************| 87388        00:00
```

The following example demonstrates how to copy a file from a remote host to a local host:

```
$ scp remote:/tmp/816-5241.pdf /tmp
user@remote's password: password
816-5241.pdf          100% |***************************| 87388        00:00
```

Using Identity Keys

This section contains examples of generating, registering, and using user identities. Agents for passphrase-free logins are also covered.

Generating an Identity

Note – OpenSSH has no default key type. The key type must be specified. The Solaris Secure Shell software defaults to Protocol 2 RSA keys.

The following example shows how to generate Protocol 2 RSA keys:

```
$ ssh-keygen -t rsa
Enter file in which to save the key(/home/user/.ssh/id_rsa):
Generating public/private rsa key pair.
Enter passphrase(empty for no passphrase): passphrase
Enter same passphrase again: passphrase
Your identification has been saved in /home/user/.ssh/id_rsa.
Your public key has been saved in /home/user/.ssh/id_rsa.pub.
The key fingerprint is:
md5 1024 f9:42:d4:0a:af:23:26:22:14:23:4a:8c:22:14:6f:f7 user@host
```

The following example shows how to generate a 2048-bit DSA key:

```
$ ssh-keygen -t dsa -b 2048
Enter file in which to save the key(/home/user/.ssh/id_dsa):
Generating public/private dsa key pair.
Enter passphrase(empty for no passphrase): passphrase
Enter same passphrase again: passphrase
Your identification has been saved in /home/user/.ssh/id_dsa.
Your public key has been saved in /home/user/.ssh/id_dsa.pub.
The key fingerprint is:
md5 2048 3c:dd:5a:8a:37:60:89:ff:ef:4a:bb:b5:bf:37:d5:78 user@host
```

The following example shows how to generate a Secure Shell Protocol 1 RSA key:

```
$ ssh-keygen -t rsa1
Enter file in which to save the key(/home/user/.ssh/identity):
Generating public/private rsa1 key pair.
Enter passphrase(empty for no passphrase): passphrase
Enter same passphrase again: passphrase
Your identification has been saved in /home/user/.ssh/identity.
Your public key has been saved in /home/user/.ssh/identity.pub.
The key fingerprint is:
md5 1024 de:30:33:84:45:1d:5d:f5:e7:84:30:58:be:b5:28:44 user@host
```

Registering an Identity

Install the generated public key into the authorized_keys file on the destination host, as in the following example. The private key is installed on the originating host of the connection.

```
$ cd ~/.ssh
$ touch authorized_keys
$ chmod 744 authorized_keys
$ cat id_rsa.pub >> authorized_keys
```

Using the Identity

The following example shows how to use the key:

```
$ ssh remote
Enter passphrase for key '/home/user/.ssh/id_rsa': passphrase
Last login: Thu Dec 19 16:48:43 2002 from server
Sun Microsystems Inc.   SunOS 5.9        Generic May 2002
remote $
```

Using Agents

This section contains examples of how to set up agents, use agent keys, and stop the agent. The following commands are used:

- ssh-agent(1)
- ssh-add(1)

Setting Up Agents

The following example shows how to set up an agent within the parent shell:

```
$ eval `ssh-agent`
Agent pid 16867
$
```

Loading Agents

The following example shows the default behavior when loading all of the identities that are present in the $HOME/.ssh directory:

```
$ ssh-add
Enter passphrase for /home/user/.ssh/id_rsa: passphrase
Identity added: /home/user/.ssh/id_rsa (/home/user/.ssh/id_rsa)
Enter passphrase for /home/user/.ssh/id_dsa: passphrase
Identity added: /home/user/.ssh/id_dsa (/home/user/.ssh/id_dsa)
```

The following example shows how to add a specific identity:

```
$ ssh-add .ssh/remote
Enter passphrase for .ssh/remote: passphrase
Identity added: .ssh/remote (.ssh/remote)
```

Listing Agent Identities

The command for listing agent identities is the same, no matter how many identities have been loaded—only the output changes.

The following example shows the output for listing an empty agent:

```
$ ssh-add -l
The agent has no identities.
```

The following example shows the output for listing an agent with one identity loaded:

```
$ ssh-add -l
md5 1024 13:cd:f7:19:87:4c:8e:5d:6c:c2:cc:51:07:af:d2:21
/home/user/.ssh/id_rsa(RSA)
```

Removing Agent Identities

The following example shows how to unload a specific identity:

```
$ ssh-add -d id_rsa
Identity removed: id_rsa(id_rsa.pub)
```

The following example shows how to unload all of the identities in an agent:

```
$ ssh-add -D
All identities removed.
```

Stopping the Agent

The following example shows how to stop an agent. Use eval(1) to unset the two shell variables.

```
$ ssh-agent -k
unset SSH_AUTH_SOCK;
unset SSH_AGENT_PID;
echo Agent pid 16867 killed;
```

Forwarding Ports

Note – The Solaris Secure Shell software defaults to having port forwarding disabled on the server.

The following example shows a local forward failing because port forwarding is disabled on the server:

```
$ telnet localhost 2020
Trying 127.0.0.1...
Connected to localhost.
Escape character is '^]'.
Connection to localhost closed by foreign host.
```

Setting Up Local Forwarding

The form for local forwarding is ssh -L *local_port:destination_host:destination_port host*. The destination host for the forwarded port does not need to be the same as port on the Secure Shell server. The following example shows the forwarding of the local host port, 2020, to the remote host's port, 23 (Telnet):

```
$ ssh -L 2020:remote:23 remote
Enter passphrase for key '/home/beth/.ssh/id_rsa': passphrase
Last login: Thu Dec 19 20:12:14 2002 from server
Sun Microsystems Inc.   SunOS 5.9        Generic May 2002
remote $
```

The following example shows how to test the forwarded port:

```
$ telnet localhost 2020
Trying 127.0.0.1...
Connected to localhost.
Escape character is '^]'.


SunOS 5.9
login: name
Password: password
Last login: Thu Dec 19 20:14:05 from server
Sun Microsystems Inc.   SunOS 5.9        Generic May 2002
remote $
```

Setting Up Remote Forwarding

The form for remote forwarding ssh -R *server_port:destination_host:destination_port
server*. The destination host does not have to be the Secure Shell server. It is often the
originating host. The following example shows the forwarding of the server's port,
2020, to port 23 (Telnet):

```
$ ssh -R 2020:remote:23 remote
Enter passphrase for key '/home/user/.ssh/id_rsa': passphrase
Last login: Thu Dec 19 20:34:25 2002 from server
Sun Microsystems Inc.   SunOS 5.9      Generic May 2002
remote /home/user $ telnet localhost 2020
Trying 127.0.0.1...
Connected to localhost.
Escape character is '^]'.
login: user
Password: password
Last login: Tue Dec 17 21:16:25 from remote
Sun Microsystems Inc.   SunOS 5.9      Generic May 2002
server $
```

Enabling X Forwarding

Note – The Solaris Secure Shell software defaults to having X forwarding disabled
on the server.

The following example shows how to enable X forwarding by adding the following
lines to the ~/.ssh/config file:

```
ForwardX11 yes
XAuthLocation /usr/X/bin/xauth
```

The following example shows how to enable X forwarding by using the -X option:

```
$ ssh -X host
```

Checking the $DISPLAY Variable

The following example shows how to check the $DISPLAY variable:

```
$ echo $DISPLAY
:0.0
$ ssh remote
Enter passphrase for key '/home/user/.ssh/id_rsa': passphrase
Last login: Thu Dec 19 19:42:30 2002 from server
Sun Microsystems Inc.    SunOS 5.9        Generic May 2002
remote $ echo $DISPLAY
remote:10.0
```

Using Proxies

Note – The ssh-http-proxy-connect(1) command and the ssh-socks5-proxy-connect(1) command are available only in the Solaris Secure Shell software.

The following example shows how to use a proxy:

```
$ ssh -o'ProxyCommand=/usr/lib/ssh/ssh-socks5-proxy-connect \
-h socks-gw -p 1080 dmz.foo.com 22' dmz.foo.com
user@dmz's password: password
Last login: Thu Dec 10 23:03:04 2002 from foo.bar.com
Sun Microsystems Inc.    SunOS 5.8        Generic May 2001
$
```

Locating Client Configuration Files

The individual client configuration file and keys are kept in the .ssh directory in the user's home directory. The global client configuration file, ssh_config, resides with the other server configuration files and keys.

The following example shows the contents of the ~/.ssh directory:

```
/home/user/.ssh $ ls -al
total 48
drwxr-xr-x    2 user   staff      512 Dec 10 10:27 .
drwxr-xr-x   26 user   other     2560 Dec 18 10:32 ..
-rw-r--r--    1 user   staff      225 Dec 10 10:27 authorized_keys
-rw-r--r--    1 user   staff      995 Dec 14 17:06 config
-rw-------    1 user   staff      951 Dec 10 10:26 id_rsa
-rw-r--r--    1 user   staff      225 Dec 10 10:26 id_rsa.pub
-rw-r--r--    1 user   staff     2325 Dec 18 12:51 known_hosts
```

Server Usage

This section covers the server-side usage of Secure Shell. The basics of starting and stopping the daemon, regenerating host keys, and using TCP Wrappers support are covered. Examples are used to demonstrate the various features. This is meant to be a brief introduction, not an in-depth guide.

Starting the Server

The following example shows how to start the Solaris Secure Shell daemon:

```
# /etc/init.d/sshd start
```

The following example shows how to start OpenSSH:

```
# /etc/init.d/openssh.server start
```

Stopping the Server

The following example shows how to stop the Solaris Secure Shell daemon:

```
# /etc/init.d/sshd stop
```

The following example shows how to stop OpenSSH:

```
# /etc/init.d/openssh.server stop
```

Locating Server Configuration Files

For the Solaris Secure Shell software, the server configuration files and keys are stored in the /etc/ssh directory.

```
$ ls -al /etc/ssh
total 30
drwxr-xr-x   2 root      sys            512 Nov 26 15:35 .
drwxr-xr-x  53 root      sys           3584 Dec  9 13:26 ..
-rw-r--r--   1 root      sys            861 Nov 26 15:02 ssh_config
-rw-------   1 root      root           668 Nov 26 15:35 ssh_host_dsa_key
-rw-r--r--   1 root      root           602 Nov 26 15:35 ssh_host_dsa_key.pub
-rw-------   1 root      root           883 Nov 26 15:35 ssh_host_rsa_key
-rw-r--r--   1 root      root           222 Nov 26 15:35 ssh_host_rsa_key.pub
-rw-r--r--   1 root      sys           5119 Nov 26 15:02 sshd_config
```

For OpenSSH, the server configuration files and keys are placed in various locations, determined by the configuration of OpenSSH at buildtime. The usual locations are the /etc, /etc/openssh, or /usr/local/etc directory. The configuration file for PRNGD could also be present.

The following example shows the contents of the /etc/openssh directory:

```
$ ls -al /etc/openssh
total 46
drwxr-xr-x   2 root      other       512 Dec 13 21:34 .
drwxr-xr-x  28 root      sys        3072 Dec 13 21:33 ..
lrwxrwxrwx   1 root      other        35 Dec 13 21:33 prngd.conf ->
/etc/openssh/prngd.conf-solaris-2.7
-rw-------   1 root      other       946 Dec 13 18:16 prngd.conf-solaris-2.6
-rw-------   1 root      other      2141 Dec 13 18:16 prngd.conf-solaris-2.7
-rw-r--r--   1 root      other      1144 Dec 13 18:16 ssh_config
-rw-------   1 root      other       668 Dec 13 21:34 ssh_host_dsa_key
-rw-r--r--   1 root      other       602 Dec 13 21:34 ssh_host_dsa_key.pub
-rw-------   1 root      other       527 Dec 13 21:34 ssh_host_key
-rw-r--r--   1 root      other       331 Dec 13 21:34 ssh_host_key.pub
-rw-------   1 root      other       883 Dec 13 21:34 ssh_host_rsa_key
-rw-r--r--   1 root      other       222 Dec 13 21:34 ssh_host_rsa_key.pub
-rw-r--r--   1 root      other      2330 Dec 13 18:16 ssh_prng_cmds
-rw-r--r--   1 root      other      2464 Dec 13 21:35 sshd_config
```

Generating New Server Host Keys

Generating new server host keys is a three-step process. First, the Secure Shell server must be stopped. Second, the existing keys must be deleted. Third, the Secure Shell server must be restarted, as in the following example:

```
# /etc/init.d/sshd stop
# cd config_directory
# rm ssh_host*
# /etc/init.d/sshd start
```

Note – Generating new server host keys will cause clients with the existing hosts key to display an error message when connecting to the host. The message will persist until the clients are updated with the new host key.

Supporting TCP Wrappers

See hosts_access(4) for details on the format for the /etc/hosts.allow and /etc/hosts.deny files.

Note – TCP Wrappers support is optional in OpenSSH. See "TCP Wrappers" on page 33 for instructions on its inclusion.

The following example shows how to allow only local network hosts access by setting up the hosts.deny and hosts.allow files:

```
# echo "sshd: ALL" >> /etc/hosts.deny
# echo "sshd: LOCAL" >> /etc/hosts.allow
```

This example shows how to test local access:

```
$ ssh server
user@server's password: password
Last login: Tue Dec 17 21:15:07 2002 from some.place
Sun Microsystems Inc.    SunOS 5.8        Generic Patch     October 2001
server /home/user $ ^D
Connection to server closed.
```

This example shows how to test remote access by attempting a connection from a remote host outside of the server's local domain:

```
$ ssh server.remote
ssh_exchange_identification: Connection closed by remote host
```

Server Configuration Options

This appendix contains a list of the server configuration options supported by the Solaris Secure Shell software and OpenSSH. The list is formatted in the following manner:

Name of the option and the value or values it takes

- Description
- Default in the Solaris Secure Shell software and OpenSSH
- Recommendation, as applicable
- References, as applicable
- Example, given in a code box

Note – Server options override the client's configuration.

AllowGroups *pattern*

- Specifies a group access control list. After authentication, access is granted if the user's primary group matches the pattern given. The primary group is the GID field listed in /etc/passwd. The pattern is the token listed in /etc/group. Wildcards of asterisk (*), matching any number of characters, or question mark (?), matching a single character, can be used. Patterns are space delimited. Use only one of the following access control keywords in the server configuration file: AllowGroups, AllowUser, DenyGroups, or DenyUsers.
- The Solaris Secure Shell software and OpenSSH default to allow access.

- See also `AllowUser`, `DenyGroups`, and `DenyUser`.

```
# Allow only the sysadmins access
AllowGroups sysadmin
```

```
# Allow both staff and sysadmin access
AllowGroups s*
```

AllowUsers *pattern*

- Specifies a user access control list. After authentication, access is granted if the user's login matches the pattern given. The pattern can be alphanumeric, but not the numerical UID value. Wildcards of asterisk (`*`), matching any number of characters, or question mark (`?`), matching a single character, can be used. Patterns are space delimited. Use only one of the following access control keywords in the server configuration file: `AllowGroups`, `AllowUser`, `DenyGroups`, or `DenyUsers`.
- The Solaris Secure Shell software and OpenSSH default to allow access.
- See also `AllowGroups`, `DenyGroups`, and `DenyUser`.

```
# Allow only Suzie and Buster access.
AllowUsers suzie buster
```

AllowTCPForwarding yes|no

- Specifies whether or not TCP forwarding (also known as port forwarding) is allowed.
- The Solaris Secure Shell software defaults to no. OpenSSH defaults to yes.
- If you want users to protect their mail, Web, or other traffic, enable this option. Setting `UseLogin` to yes in OpenSSH disables this feature.
- See also `GatewayPorts` and `X11Forwarding`.

Note – If users have shell access, they can install their own port forwarders. If this is an issue, consider RBAC to limit access.

```
# Protect user's traffic
AllowTCPForwarding yes
```

```
# Only allow a remote job restricted access to gather logs.
AllowTCPForwarding no
```

Banner *value*

- Specifies a banner that is displayed along with the authentication prompt. If your environment requires this banner, set to /etc/issue so that only one banner exists for the entire system.

- The Solaris Secure Shell software and OpenSSH default to no banner.

```
Banner /etc/issue
```

The following example shows a connection with the sample banner from the Solaris Security Toolkit software.

```
hook /home/suzi $ ssh blackbeard

|-------------------------------------------------------------------|
| This system is for the use of authorized users only.              |
| Individuals using this computer system without authority, or in   |
| excess of their authority, are subject to having all of their     |
| activities on this system monitored and recorded by system       |
| personnel.                                                        |
|                                                                   |
| In the course of monitoring individuals improperly using this    |
| system, or in the course of system maintenance, the activities   |
| of authorized users may also be monitored.                       |
|                                                                   |
| Anyone using this system expressly consents to such monitoring    |
| and is advised that if such monitoring reveals possible           |
| evidence of criminal activity, system personnel may provide the   |
| evidence of such monitoring to law enforcement officials.         |
|-------------------------------------------------------------------|

suzi@blackbeard's password: password
Last login: Wed Feb 5 14:41:01 2003 from hook
Sun Microsystems Inc.    SunOS 5.9      Generic May 2002
blackbeard /home/suzi $
```

CheckMail yes|no

- Specifies whether or not the server should check for new mail. In the Solaris OE, the login shell should check for new mail only during the beginning of interactive logins.

- The Solaris Secure Shell software defaults to no. New versions of OpenSSH no longer honor this keyword.

- Recommended value is no.

- See also `PrintMotd`.

```
CheckMail no
```

Ciphers *list*

- For Protocol 2 only, specifies which ciphers are available. The cipher list is comma delimited, and the clients use the first available choice, unless overridden on the command line.

- The Solaris Secure Shell software defaults to `aes128-cbc,blowfish-cbc,3des-cbc`. OpenSSH defaults to `aes128-cbc,3des-cbc,blowfish-cbc,cast128-cbc,arcfour,aes192-cbc,aes256-cbc`.

```
Ciphers aes128-cbc,blowfish-cbc,3des-cbc
```

Compression yes|no

- Specifies whether or not compression can be used.

- The Solaris Secure Shell software and OpenSSH default to yes.

- Recommended value is yes.

```
Compression yes
```

DenyGroups *pattern*

- Specifies a group access control list. After authentication, access is denied if the user's primary group matches the given pattern. The primary group is the GID field listed in /etc/passwd. The pattern is the token listed in /etc/group. Wildcards of asterisk (*), matching any number of characters, or question mark

(?), matching a single character, can be used. Patterns are space delimited. Use only one of the following access control keywords in the server configuration file: AllowGroups, AllowUser, DenyGroups, or DenyUsers.

- The Solaris Secure Shell software and OpenSSH default to allow access.

- See also AllowGroups, AllowUsers, and DenyUsers.

```
# Prevent the users from logging in to the server
DenyGroups users
```

DenyUsers *pattern*

- Specifies a user access control list. After authentication, access is denied if the user's login matches the pattern given. The pattern can be alphanumeric, but not the numerical UID value. Wildcards of asterisk (*), matching any number of characters, or question mark (?), matching a single character, can be used. Patterns are space delimited. Use only one of the following access control keywords in the server configuration file: AllowGroups, AllowUser, DenyGroups, or DenyUsers.

- The Solaris Secure Shell software and OpenSSH default to allow access.

- See also AllowGroups, AllowUsers, and DenyGroups.

```
DenyUsers Cheng Atkinson
```

DSAAuthentication yes|no

- For Protocol 2 only, specifies whether or not DSA authentication is allowed.

- The Solaris Secure Shell software and OpenSSH default to yes.

- Recommended value is yes.

- See also PubKeyAuthentication.

```
DSAAuthentication yes
```

GatewayPorts yes|no

- Specifies whether or not remote hosts are allowed to connect to ports forwarded by the client. This can be used to form a limited VPN setup. Setting UseLogin to yes in OpenSSH disables this feature.

- The Solaris Secure Shell software and OpenSSH default to no.

- Recommended value is no.

Note – Users can chain together port forwarders (that is, create a bouncer) on the local machine to circumvent this restriction.

- See also `AllowTCPForwarding`.

```
GatewayPorts no
```

HostKey *value*

- Specifies the private host key files. These keys are used to securely identify the server. `ssh_host_key` is needed for Protocol 1 support. `ssh_host_rsa_key` is needed for Protocol 2 RSA authentication. `ssh_host_dsa_key` is needed for Protocol 2 DSA authentication. The keys must be generated with `ssh-keygen` if they do not exist before first invocation of `sshd(1M)`.
- The Solaris Secure Shell software defaults to: `/etc/ssh`
  OpenSSH defaults to: `/usr/local/etc`

```
HostKey /etc/ssh/ssh_host_key
HostKey /etc/ssh/ssh_host_rsa_key
HostKey /etc/ssh/ssh_host_dsa_key
```

IgnoreRhosts yes|no

- For Protocol 1 only, specifies whether or not a user's `.rhosts` and `.shosts` files are used for authentication.
- The Solaris Secure Shell software and OpenSSH default to no.
- Recommended value is yes.
- See also `RhostsAuthentication`.

```
IgnoreRhosts yes
```

IgnoreUserKnownHosts yes|no

- For Protocol 1, specifies whether or not a user's `~/.ssh/known_hosts` file will be used during `RhostsRSAAuthentication`.
- The Solaris Secure Shell software and OpenSSH default to no.

- Recommended value is yes.
- See also RhostsRSAAuthentication.

```
IgnoreUserKnownHosts yes
```

KeepAlive yes|no

- Specifies whether or not TCP keep-alives are sent. If they are sent, the death of a connection, crash of a machine, or downing of a route will be noticed, and the connection terminated. This prevents connections from hanging and consuming resources.
- The Solaris Secure Shell software and OpenSSH default to yes.
- Recommended value is yes.

```
KeepAlive yes
```

KeyRegenerationInterval *value*

- For Protocol 1 only, the ephemeral key (that is, the key to encrypt data, not the one to identify the server) is regenerated after the designated time in seconds, if it has been used.
- The Solaris Secure Shell software and OpenSSH default to 3600 seconds.
- Recommend value is 1800 seconds. Do not set this value too low, or the server will spend all of its time generating new keys.

```
KeyRegenerationInterval 1800
```

ListenAddress *value*

- Specifies the local address on which the server should listen. For multihomed machines, you can limit the server to listening on only one address. The Port keyword must be placed before this keyword.
- The Solaris Secure Shell software and OpenSSH default to listen to all local addresses.

- Recommended value is to limit to only administrative address interfaces, when possible.

```
ListenAddress 192.168.0.5
```

LoginGraceTime *value*

- Specifies the grace time during which a connection can exist without successful authentication.
- The Solaris Secure Shell software defaults to 600 seconds.
- OpenSSH defaults to 120 seconds.
- Recommended value is 60 seconds.
- See also MaxStartups.

```
LoginGraceTime 60
```

LogLevel *value*

- Specifies the verbosity of logging information. Information is logged by using syslog(3). Higher levels generate a larger volume of log data.
- The Solaris Secure Shell software and OpenSSH default to INFO.
- See also SyslogFacility.
- See syslog(3), syslog.conf(4), and syslogd(1M) for information.

```
LogLevel DEBUG
```

MACs *list*

- For Protocol 2 only, specifies which message authentication code (MAC) algorithms are available. The MAC list is comma delimited. The clients use the first match, unless overridden on the command line.
- The Solaris Secure Shell software defaults to hmac-sha1, hmac-md5. OpenSSH defaults to hmac-md5, hmac-sha1, hmac-ripemd160, hmac-sha1-96, hmac-md5-96.

```
MACS hmac-sha1,hmac-md5
```

MaxAuthTries *value*

- For the Solaris Secure Shell software only, specifies the maximum number of retries for authentication before a connection is dropped.
- The default is 6. This value cannot be overridden by `ConnectionAttempts` in the client configuration file.

```
MaxAuthTries 6
```

The following is an example of when `MaxAuthTries` is set to 2, and the user fails to log in successfully:

```
hook /home/suzi $ ssh blackbeard
suzi@blackbeard's password: password
Permission denied, please try again.
suzi@blackbeard's password: password
Received disconnect: 2: too many failed userauth_requests
hook /home/suzi $
```

MaxAuthTriesLog *value*

- For the Solaris Secure Shell software only, specifies the number of retries for authentication before a warning message is logged.
- The default is `MaxAuthTries` divided by two.
- See also `LogLevel` and `SyslogFacility`.

```
MaxAuthTriesLog 3
```

MaxStartups *value*

- Specifies the maximum number of concurrent unauthenticated connections. When the limit is reached, no new connections are allowed until the count drops.
- The Solaris Secure Shell software and OpenSSH default to 10.
- See also `LoginGraceTime`.

```
MaxStartups 10
```

PAMAuthenticationViaKBDInt yes|no

- Specifies whether or not to use pluggable authentication modules through the keyboard interactive method for authentication. Setting the value to yes allows the use of custom pluggable authentication modules.
- The Solaris Secure Shell software and OpenSSH default to yes.
- Recommended value is yes.

```
PAMAuthenticationViaKBDInt yes
```

PasswordAuthentication yes|no

- Specifies whether or not passwords can be used for authentication. For systems with many users on internal corporate accounts, password authentication is sufficient. For remote users or automated execution, use key-based authentication.
- The Solaris Secure Shell software and OpenSSH default to yes.
- See also PermitEmptyPasswords, PermitRootLogin, and PubKeyAuthentication.

```
# Internal mail server
PasswordAuthentication yes
```

```
# DMZ Bastion host
PasswordAuthentication no
```

PermitEmptyPasswords yes|no

- Specifies whether or not accounts with empty passwords are allowed to log in.
- The Solaris Secure Shell software and OpenSSH default to no.
- Recommended value is no.
- See also PasswordAuthentication.

```
PermitEmptyPasswords no
```

PermitRootLogin yes | no | without-password | forced-commands-only

- Specifies whether or not the superuser (root) account can log in over the network. without-password allows logins by using key-based authentication only. For OpenSSH only, the additional value, forced-commands-only, can be used. This requires key-based authentication and a command to be associated with the particular key.
- The Solaris Secure Shell software defaults to no. OpenSSH defaults to yes.
- Recommended value is no.
- See also PasswordAuthentication and PubKeyAuthentication.

```
# Force the system admins to su
PermitRootLogin no
```

```
# Only a root account exists
PermitRootLogin without-password
```

PermitUserEnvironment yes | no

- For OpenSSH only, specifies whether or not the server should process environment options in ~/.ssh/environment or ~/.ssh/authorized keys.
- The default and recommended value is no.

```
PermitUserEnvironment no
```

Port value

- Specifies the port on which the server is to listen. The Internet Assigned Numbers Authority (IANA) assigned port for Secure Shell is 22. If your firewall blocks low-value ports (less than 1024), a higher value might be needed. You can have multiple listings of this keyword.
- The Solaris Secure Shell software and OpenSSH default to 22.

```
# For LAN access
Port 22
# For Internet access
Port 2345
```

PrintMotd yes|no

- Specifies whether or not the server should display the message-of-the-day (MOTD). In the Solaris OE, the login shell should display the MOTD at the beginning of interactive logins.
- The Solaris Secure Shell software defaults to no. OpenSSH defaults to yes.
- Recommended value is no.
- See also CheckMail.

```
PrintMotd no
```

Protocol *list*

- Specifies the Secure Shell protocols available. The first version of the protocol has been deprecated because of flaws in the protocol allowed packet insertion and password length-determination attacks. The second version of the protocol was developed to address the problems. The client uses the first available protocol in the list.
- The Solaris Secure Shell software defaults to 2. OpenSSH defaults to 2,1.
- Recommended value is 2.

```
# Protocol 2 only is recommended
Protocol 2
```

```
# Enable legacy support but default to Protocol 2.
Protocol 2,1
```

PubKeyAuthentication yes|no

- Specifies whether or not public keys can be used for authentication.
- The Solaris Secure Shell software and OpenSSH default to yes.
- Recommended value is yes.
- See also PasswordAuthentication.

```
PubKeyAuthentication yes
```

RhostsAuthentication yes|no

- For protocol 1 only, specifies whether or not rhosts(4) or hosts.equiv(4) authentication is sufficient.
- The Solaris Secure Shell software and OpenSSH default to no.
- Recommended value is no.
- See also IgnoreRhosts.

```
RhostsAuthentication no
```

RhostsRSAAuthentication yes|no

- For Protocol 1 only, specifies whether or not rhosts(4) or hosts.equiv(4) authentication with RSA host authentication is allowed.
- The Solaris Secure Shell software and OpenSSH default to no.
- Recommended value is no.
- See also IgnoreUserKnownHosts.

```
RhostsRSAAuthentication no
```

RSAAuthentication yes|no

- For Protocol 1 only, specifies whether or not RSA Protocol 1 user authentication is allowed.
- The Solaris Secure Shell software and OpenSSH default to yes.
- Recommended value is yes.

```
RSAAuthentication yes
```

ServerKeyBits *value*

- For Protocol 1 only, this is the size in bits of the server key.
- The Solaris Secure Shell software and OpenSSH default to 768.
- Recommended value is 1024.

```
ServerKeyBits 1024
```

StrictModes yes|no

- In case a user's home directory or .ssh files are world writable or if they are owned by someone else, the server will prevent a login. This action prevents a compromise.
- The Solaris Secure Shell software and OpenSSH default to yes.
- Recommended value is yes.

```
StrictModes yes
```

SyslogFacility *value.value*

- Specifies the facility and security codes to use when logging by using syslog(3).
- The Solaris Secure Shell software and OpenSSH default to AUTH.INFO.
- See also LogLevel.
- Consult syslog(3), syslog.conf(4), and syslogd(1M) for more information.

```
SyslogFacility AUTH.INFO
```

UseLogin yes|no

- For OpenSSH only, specifies whether or not login(1) is called for interactive sessions. This feature is required for BSM auditing. Turning it on will disable X11 and port forwarding. cron(1M) will also partially break. See "Auditing" on page 81 for details on the consequences of UseLogin and on getting BSM auditing to work successfully. This feature will not work if UsePrivilegeSeparation is set to yes.
- The default value is no.
- Recommended value is no.

```
UseLogin no
```

UsePrivilegeSeparation yes|no

- For OpenSSH only, specifies whether or not the server separates privileges by having an unprivileged child process deal with incoming network traffic. After successful authentication, a separate process is created with the privileges of the user. This is an attempt to prevent a root compromise by any corruption from the incoming network traffic (for example, a buffer overflow). This feature does not work with pluggable authentication modules on the Solaris OE.

Note – The compilations options presented in Chapter 2 disable this feature.

- The default value is yes.
- Recommended value is no.

```
UsePrivilegeSeparation no
```

X11DisplayOffset *value*

- Specifies the first display number available for the server's X11 forwarding. This option prevents interference with real X11 servers.
- The Solaris Secure Shell software and OpenSSH default to 10. For Sun Ray™ appliance servers, if this value is too low, increase by the maximum number of clients, plus a margin for error.

```
# For desktops or server
X11DisplayOffset 10
```

```
# For Sun Ray appliance servers, may need to be more.
X11DisplayOffset 100
```

X11Forwarding yes|no

- Specifies whether or not X11 forwarding is permitted. In OpenSSH, setting UseLogin to yes disables this feature. If you want users to protect their X11 traffic, enable this option.
- The Solaris Secure Shell software and OpenSSH default to no.

Note – Users with shell access can install their own X11 forwarders. If this is an issue, consider RBAC to limit access. For Solaris 9 OE systems, consider using X with the -nolisten flag to limit exposure. This flag limits the X11 applications to running only on the server.

- See also `AllowTCPForwarding`.

```
# Protect user's X sessions
X11Forwarding yes
```

```
# Only allow restricted access for a remote job
X11Forwarding no
```

XAuthLocation *value*

- Specifies the location of the `xauth(1)` program. This option will not override the default that is used when the software is compiled.
- The Solaris Secure Shell software defaults to: `/usr/X/bin/xauth` OpenSSH defaults to: `/usr/openwin/bin/xauth`
- Recommended value is: `/usr/X/bin/xauth`

```
XAuthLocation /usr/X/bin/xauth
```

Client Configuration Options

This appendix contains a list of the client configuration options supported by the Solaris Secure Shell software and OpenSSH. The list is formatted in the following manner:

Name of the option and the value or values it takes

- Description
- Default in the Solaris Secure Shell software and OpenSSH
- Recommendation, as applicable
- References, as applicable
- Example, given in a code box

Note – Client options cannot override the server's configuration.

BatchMode yes|no

- Specifies whether or not the password or passphrase prompting is disabled. Use this option in scripts for automated logins.
- The Solaris Secure Shell software and OpenSSH default to no.

```
# For automated scripts
BatchMode yes
```

CheckHostIP yes|no

- Specifies whether or not to check the server IP address in the known_hosts file. This option detects DNS spoofing.

- The Solaris Secure Shell software and OpenSSH default to yes.
- Recommended value is yes.
- See also `StrictHostKeyChecking`.

```
CheckHostIP yes
```

Cipher 3des|blowfish|des

- For Protocol 1 only, specifies the ciphers to use when encrypting the session, in order of preference. Multiple ciphers are comma delimited.
- The Solaris Secure Shell software and OpenSSH default to `3des`. `des` is supported only on OpenSSH.
- Recommended value is `3des`.
- See also `Ciphers`.

```
# For legacy protocol 1 servers only
Cipher 3des,blowfish
```

Ciphers *list*

- For Protocol 2 only, specifies the ciphers to use when encrypting the session, in order of preference. Multiple ciphers are comma delimited.
- The Solaris Secure Shell software defaults to `3des-cbc,blowfish-cbc,aes-128-cbc`. OpenSSH defaults to `aes128-cbc,3des-cbc,blowfish-cbc,cast128-cbc,arcfour,aes192-cbc,aes256-cbc`.
- See also `Cipher`.

```
Ciphers 3des-cbc,blowfish-cbc,aes-128-cbc
```

Compression yes|no

- Specifies whether or not to use compression. Compression can improve performance over low-bandwidth network connections. No performance will be gained in the transfer of minimally compressible data such as MPEG2 files or GZIP compressed files.
- The Solaris Secure Shell software and OpenSSH default to no.
- Recommended value is yes, if transferring a large amount of text data (for example, logs).

- See also `CompressionLevel`.

```
Compression yes
```

CompressionLevel *value*

- Specifies the compression level to use. Valid values are 1 (least compression, but fastest performance) through 9 (most compression, but slowest performance). This keyword requires `Compression` set to yes.
- The Solaris Secure Shell software and OpenSSH default to 6.
- See also `Compression`.

```
CompressionLevel 9
```

ConnectionAttempts *value*

- Specifies the number of attempts to make a connection before exiting or falling back to `rsh(1)`.
- The Solaris Secure Shell software and OpenSSH default to 3.
- See also `FallbackToRsh` and `NumberOfPasswordPrompts`.

```
ConnectionAttempts 3
```

DSAAuthentication yes│no

- For Protocol 2 only, specifies whether or not to attempt DSA authentication. This option requires a DSA identity file.
- The Solaris Secure Shell software and OpenSSH default to yes.
- Recommended value is yes.
- See also `PasswordAuthentication` and `PubkeyAuthentication`.

```
DSAAuthentication yes
```

EscapeChar *Value*

- Specifies the escape character. Valid values are a single character or a caret (^) followed by a character to symbolize a control character. The value can also be left empty to have no escape character.
- The Solaris Secure Shell software and OpenSSH default to tilde (~).

```
# Completely transparent connection
EscapeChar
```

FallBackToRsh yes|no

- Specifies whether or not the client should use rsh(1) if it is unable to make a secure connection.
- The Solaris Secure Shell software and OpenSSH default to no.
- Recommended value is no.
- See also ConnectionAttempts and UseRsh.

```
FallBackToRsh no
```

ForwardAgent yes|no

- Specifies whether or not the agent connection will be forwarded to the server.
- The Solaris Secure Shell software and OpenSSH default to no.
- Recommended value is no.

```
ForwardAgent no
```

ForwardX11 yes|no

- Specifies whether or not to enable X11 connection forwarding.
- The Solaris Secure Shell software defaults to no. OpenSSH defaults to yes.
- Recommended value is yes if users need to protect X connections.

```
ForwardX11 yes
```

GatewayPorts yes|no

- Specifies whether or not other hosts may use forwarded ports.
- The Solaris Secure Shell software and OpenSSH default to no.
- Recommended value is no.
- See also `LocalForward` and `RemoteForward`.

```
GatewayPorts no
```

GlobalKnownHostsFile *value*

- Specifies global known host file, other than the default.
- The Solaris Secure Shell software defaults to: `/etc/ssh_known_hosts`
  OpenSSH defaults to: `/usr/local/etc/ssh_known_hosts`
- See also `UserKnownHostsFile`.

```
GlobalKnownHostsFile /etc/ssh_known_hosts
```

Host *value*

- Restricts keyword designations to a particular host until the next `Host` keyword. The `Host` value is given on the command line. Wildcards of asterisk (*), matching any number of characters, or question mark (?), matching a single character, can be used. An asterisk by itself is used to set global defaults.
- See also `HostName`.

```
# Only for legacy host
Host legacy
Protocol 1
# defaults
Host *
Protocol 2
CheckHostIP yes
ConnectionAttempts 3
```

HostName *value*

- Specifies the real host name to which to connect. Allows abbreviations or nicknames to be specified on the command line. Numeric IP addresses are also allowed. Use with the `Host` keyword.
- See also `Host`.

```
Host legacy
HostName legacy.extremefoosticks.com.
Protocol 1
```

IdentityFile *value*

- Specifies the file from which to read identities. Multiple listings can be given that will be checked sequentially.
- The Solaris Secure Shell software and OpenSSH default to `~/.ssh/identity` for Protocol 1, `~/.ssh/id_rsa` for RSA authentication in Protocol 2, and `~/.ssh/id_dsa` for DSA authentication in Protocol 2.

```
IdentityFile ~/.ssh/dsa_ident_2
```

KeepAlive yes|no

- Specifies whether or not TCP keep-alives are sent. If they are sent, the death of a connection, crash of a machine, or downing of a route will be noticed, and the connection will be terminated. This option prevents connections from hanging and consuming resources.
- The Solaris Secure Shell software and OpenSSH default to `yes`.
- Recommended value is `yes`.

```
KeepAlive yes
```

LocalForward *localhost_port destination_host:port*

- Specifies that *localhost_port* be forwarded to the *destination_host* and *port* through the server. Only the superuser can forward privileged ports (numbered below1024).
- The Solaris Secure Shell software and OpenSSH default to no forwardings.

- See also `GatewayPorts` and `RemoteForward`.

```
LocalForward 8080 intranet.extremefoosticks.com:80
```

LogLevel *value*

- Specifies the level of logging from the client. Possible values are `QUIET`, `FATAL`, `ERROR`, `INFO`, `VERBOSE`, and `DEBUG`, in order of increasing verbosity. OpenSSH additionally has `DEBUG1`, `DEBUG2`, `DEBUG3`.
- The Solaris Secure Shell software and OpenSSH default to `INFO`.

```
LogLevel DEBUG
```

MACs *list*

- For Protocol 2 only, specifies which message authentication algorithm (MAC) to use in order of preference. This is a comma-delimited list.
- The Solaris Secure Shell software defaults to `hmac-sha1,hmac-md5`. OpenSSH defaults to `hmac-md5,hmac-sha1,hmac-ripemd160,hmac-sha1-96,hmac-md5-96`.

```
MACs hmac-sha1,hmac-md5
```

NumberOfPasswordPrompts *value*

- Specifies the number of password prompts allowed before exiting.
- The Solaris Secure Shell software and OpenSSH default to `3`.
- See also `ConnectionAttempts`.

```
NumberOfPasswordPrompts 3
```

PasswordAuthentication yes | no

- Specifies whether or not to attempt password authentication.
- The Solaris Secure Shell software and OpenSSH default to `yes`.

- See also `PubkeyAuthentication`.

```
PasswordAuthentication yes
```

Port *value*

- Specifies the port to connect to on the server. The port assigned to the Secure Shell by the Internet Assigned Numbers Authority (IANA) is 22.
- The Solaris Secure Shell software and OpenSSH default to 22.

```
Port 22
```

Protocol *list*

- Specifies the Secure Shell protocol to use, in order of preference. The first version of the protocol has been deprecated because flaws in the protocol allowed packet insertion and password length-determination attacks. The second version of the protocol was developed to address these problems. This is a comma-delimited list.
- The Solaris Secure Shell software and OpenSSH default to 2,1.
- Recommended value is 2.

```
# Protocol 2 only is recommended
Protocol 2
```

```
# Enable legacy support but default to Protocol 2.
Protocol 2,1
```

ProxyCommand

- Specifies an external command through which to send the Secure Shell traffic. `CheckHostIP` is ignored with `ProxyCommand`. Use with the `Host` keyword. Line breaks are not permitted in this keyword.

- The Solaris Secure Shell software provides two proxies in `/usr/lib/ssh`: `ssh-socks5-proxy-connect` and `ssh-http-proxy-connect`. Consult their respective man pages for more details.

```
Host remote
ProxyCommand /usr/lib/ssh/ssh-socks5-proxy-connect -h socks.corp -p 1080
homebox.myhome.org 22
```

PubkeyAuthentication yes | no

- For Protocol 2 only, specifies whether or not to attempt public key authentication.
- The Solaris Secure Shell software and OpenSSH default to yes.
- See also `DSAAuthentication` and `PasswordAuthentication`.

```
PubkeyAuthentication   yes
```

RemoteForward *port destination_host* : *port*

- Specifies that the *port* on the server be forwarded to the *destination_host* and *port* through the client. Only the superuser can forward privileged ports (numbered below 1024).
- The Solaris Secure Shell software and OpenSSH default to no forwardings.
- See also `LocalForward`.

```
RemoteForward 8080 www.sun.com:80
```

RhostsAuthentication yes | no

- For Protocol 1 only, specifies whether or not to attempt `rhosts(4)` authentication. This option requires OpenSSH to be installed as `setuid`.
- The Solaris Secure Shell software will not do this because it is not installed as `setuid`. OpenSSH defaults to no.
- Recommended value is no.
- See also `UsePrivilegedPort`.

```
RhostsAuthentication no
```

RhostsRSAAuthentication yes|no

- For Protocol 1 only, specifies whether or not to attempt rhosts authentication, based on RSA host keys. This option requires OpenSSH to be installed as setuid.
- The Solaris Secure Shell software will not do this because it is not installed as setuid. OpenSSH defaults to no.
- Recommended value is no.
- See also UsePrivilegedPort.

```
RhostsRSAAuthentication no
```

RSAAuthentication yes|no

- For Protocol 1 only, specifies whether or not to attempt RSA authentication, provided an identity file exists.
- The Solaris Secure Shell software and OpenSSH default to yes.
- Recommended value is yes.

```
RSAAuthentication yes
```

StrictHostKeyChecking yes|ask|no

- Specifies whether or not the client automatically adds new host keys to the known_hosts file, prompts the user, or never adds the key. In the case of yes and ask, the client will refuse to connect to a host that has a changed host key.
- The Solaris Secure Shell software and OpenSSH default to ask.
- Recommended value is yes or ask.
- See also CheckHostIP.

```
StrictHostKeyChecking   yes
```

UsePrivilegedPort yes|no

- Specifies whether or not to use a privileged port for outgoing connections. Setting to no disables RhostsAuthentication and RhostsRSAAuthentication authentication.

- The Solaris Secure Shell software will not use a privileged port. OpenSSH must be installed as `setuid` to use a privileged port.
- Recommended value is no.
- See also `RhostsAuthentication` and `RhostsRSAAuthentication`.

```
UsePrivilegedPort no
```

User *value*

- Specifies the user to authenticate. Use with the `Host` keyword.
- The Solaris Secure Shell software and OpenSSH default to the user name that invoked the client.
- See also `Host`.

```
Host legacy
User buster44
```

UserKnownHostsFile *value*

- Specifies the user `known_hosts` file, other than the default.
- The Solaris Secure Shell software and OpenSSH default to `$HOME/.ssh/known_hosts`.
- See also `GlobalKnownHostsFile`.

```
UserKnownHostsFile /home/suzi/.ssh/backup_known_hosts
```

UseRsh yes|no

- Specifies whether or not to use `rsh(1)` instead of the Secure Shell protocol. This option requires having `rsh(1)` installed on the system.
- The Solaris Secure Shell software and OpenSSH default to no.
- Recommended value is no.
- See also `FallbackToRsh`.

```
UseRsh no
```

XAuthLocation *value*

- Specifies the location of the xauth(1) program. This option will not override the default value that was used when the software was compiled.

- The Solaris Secure Shell software and OpenSSH default to: /usr/openwin/bin/xauth

- Recommended value is: /usr/X/bin/xauth

```
XAuthLocation /usr/X/bin/xauth
```

Performance Test Methodology

This appendix lists how and under what conditions the metrics from "Measuring Performance" on page 91 were obtained. The systems are detailed. The software is specified, and the data sampling techniques are documented. This information is presented for those interested in performing their own performance testing.

Bandwidth Performance

Two Netra™ ct 400 servers were used to run the tests. Each server had a single UltraSPARC™ IIi 440-MHz processor, 1024 Mbytes of memory, and a Seagate ST336704LSUN36G disk drive. The Solaris 9 12/02 OE for the SPARC platform was installed with the 64-bit SUNWCall cluster. The two servers were connected to a network switch using hme0.

The versions of telnet, rlogin, ftp, and the Solaris Secure Shell software in the Solaris 9 12/02 OE were used.

For each session, the packets were captured using snoop(1M). The packets were saved in a file to calculate the total data transferred. The packet count returned by snoop(1M) for the session was used. snoop(1M) was configured to capture only packets between the two testing hosts.

The interactive ls / session consisted of a simple login (user name and password), the display of /etc/motd, the ls / session, and its results. The interactive cat /usr/dict/words session was the same as the ls / session, except for the cat /usr/dict/words command and its results. The file transfer sessions consisted of a simple login (user name and password) and the transfer of the listed file. The Solaris 8 2/02 SPARC install-image TAR file was the same used for the Symmetric Cipher Performance measurements. The scp(1) command used the AES cipher to transfer the files.

Identity Generation

A Sun Blade™ 1000 workstation was used to run the tests. The workstation had an UltraSPARC III 750-MHz processor, 512 Mbytes of memory, and a Seagate ST336605FSUN36G hard drive. The Solaris 9 12/02 OE for the SPARC platform was installed with the 64-bit SUNWCall cluster.

The version of the Solaris Secure Shell software in the Solaris 9 12/02 OE was used.

A ksh(1) script was written that generated an identity 12 times for each type, at increasingly larger sizes (integer multiples of 512 bits) from 512 to 4096 bits. The generated identities were written to the local disk with no passphrases. The real-time data reported by the time(1) command was gathered. All of the data was entered into a StarOffice™ 6.0 spreadsheet and averaged.

The system was in the multiuser run level (3) with all of the default system daemons present. This setup did impact performance. A separate run in single-user mode (run level S after a reboot) showed increased performance (100 percent in some cases). There was a large variance in the data gathered, with the worst-case performance being three times the average performance. No effort was made to prevent entropy exhaustion. The following is the ksh(1) source fragment that generated the data:

```
for keytype in rsa1 rsa dsa do
        print "keytype : $keytype"

        for size in 512 1024 1536 2048 2560 3072 3584 4096
        do
                print "size : $size"
                for run in 1 2 3 4 5 6 7 8 9 10 11 12
                do
                        print "###"
                        time ssh-keygen -t $keytype -b $size -N "" \
                                -f ${keytype}.${size}.${run}
                        print "\n###"
                done
        done
done
```

Symmetric Cipher Performance

An Ultra™ 60 workstation was used to the build the software and run the tests. The workstation had an UltraSPARC II 450-MHz processor, 512 Mbytes of memory, and a Seagate ST336704LSUN36G disk drive.

The Solaris 8 2/02 OE for the SPARC platform was installed with the 64-bit SUNWCall cluster. Patches 112438-01 and 112611-01 were added.

The Forte Developer 7 C 5.4 software was used to build OpenSSL and OpenSSH. OpenSSL 0.9.6g was configured with the solaris-sparcv9-cc target. OpenSSH 3.5p1 was configured with the following options:

```
./configure --with-pam --disable-suid-ssh --without-rsh \
--with-lastlog=/var/adm/lastlog --sysconfdir=/etc/openssh \
--prefix=/opt/OBSDssh --without-privsep-user --without-privsep-path \
--without-prngd --with-out-rand-helper \
--with-cflags="-xO5 -xdepend -dalign -xlibmil -xunroll=5 -xprefetch "
```

A ksh(1) script was written to transfer a test file 12 times for each cipher type. The file was transferred using scp(2) in Protocol 2. The file was a Solaris 8 2/02 OE SPARC install image in TAR format at 711,000,576 bytes in size. The file was written to /dev/null. This caused an encryption by the client and a decryption by the server. The transfer was over the loopback interface. The data gathered was the time reported by the scp(1) command. The values were converted to seconds and averaged. The following is the ksh(1) source fragment that generated the data:

```
function doruns {

        $COPY -c $1 $XFER ${HOST}:/dev/null

}

for cipher in aes128-cbc blowfish-cbc 3des-cbc
do
        print "Cipher : $cipher"

        for run in 1 2 3 4 5 6 7 8 9 10 11 12
        do
                doruns $cipher
        done
done
```

Scripts and Configuration Files

This appendix contains examples of the scripts and configuration files referenced in this book. It also contains procedures for installing the scripts, when applicable. You can use these examples and procedures to set up and configure your Secure Shell environment.

`init` Script

The OpenSSH tool provides strong authentication and privacy for network connections. The `init` script in this section provides a mechanism to start and stop the OpenSSH system daemon at system boot and shutdown. This script is written for the Solaris 2.6, 7, 8, and 9 OE releases. The latest version of this script is available from the Blueprints Online tools area at:

```
http://www.sun.com/blueprints/tools/
```

Automatic Installation

The `init` script is automatically configured by `makeOpenSSHPackage.ksh`. It is installed by the resulting package installation.

Manual Installation

You can install the `init` script manually by using the following procedure.

▼ To Manually Install the `init` Script

1. Edit the `init` script by making the changes to values denoted by `%%`.

2. Copy the script to `/etc/init.d/openssh.server`.

3. Change the permissions to 744.

```
# chmod 744 /etc/init.d/openssh.server
```

4. Change the owner of the script.

```
# chown root:sys /etc/init.d/openssh.server
```

5. Create the following links:

```
# ln /etc/init.d/openssh.server /etc/rc3.d/S25openssh.server
# ln /etc/init.d/openssh.server /etc/rcS.d/K30openssh.server
# ln /etc/init.d/openssh.server /etc/rc0.d/K30openssh.server
# ln /etc/init.d/openssh.server /etc/rc1.d/K30openssh.server
# ln /etc/init.d/openssh.server /etc/rc2.d/K40openssh.server
```

Contact

For inquiries or feedback, contact `openssh_tools@sun.com`.

init Script Sample

```
#!/sbin/sh
#
#
umask 022
PATH=/usr/bin

configDir=%%configDir%%
openSSHDir=%%openSSHDir%%

usePRNGD=%%includePRNGD%%

PRNGDConfig=$configDir/prngd.conf
PRNGDEntropyDir=/var/run
PRNGDSeedFile=$PRNGDEntropyDir/prngd-seed
PRNGDEntropyPool=$PRNGDEntropyDir/egd-pool
PRNGDCmd=$openSSHDir/sbin/prngd
PRNGDCmdOptions="--cmdfile $PRNGDConfig --seedfile $PRNGDSeedFile \
          $PRNGDEntropyPool"

DSAKeyFile=$configDir/ssh_host_dsa_key
RSA2KeyFile=$configDir/ssh_host_rsa_key
RSA1KeyFile=$configDir/ssh_host_key
keyGenerator=$openSSHDir/bin/ssh-keygen

sshdConfig=$configDir/sshd_config
sshdPIDFile=sshd.pid
sshdCmd=$openSSHDir/sbin/sshd
sshdCmdOptions=""

#
# Checks for the existence of the host DSA key (protocol version 2)
#
DSAKeyExists() {
    [ -f "$DSAKeyFile" ] && return 0
    return 1
}

#
# Checks for the existence of the host RSA key (protocol version 2)
#
RSA2KeyExists() {
    [ -f "$RSA2KeyFile" ] && return 0
    return 1
}
```

```
#
# Checks for the existence of the RSA host key (protocol version 1)
#
RSA1KeyExists() {
    [ -f "$RSA1KeyFile" ] && return 0
    return 1
}


#
# Checks for the existence of the PRNGD initial seed
#
PRNGDSeedExists() {
    [ -s "$PRNGDSeedFile" ] && return 0
    return 1
}


#
# Configures the appropriate PRNGD config file
#
setPRNGDConfigFile() {
    [ ! -f "$PRNGDConfig" ] && {
        OSrev=`uname -r`
        case "$OSrev" in
            "5.7"|"5.8"|"5.9")
                ln -s $PRNGDConfig-solaris-2.7 $PRNGDConfig
                ;;
            *)
                ln -s $PRNGDConfig-solaris-2.6 $PRNGDConfig
                ;;
        esac
    }
}


#
# Generates DSA (protocol version 2) key
#
generateDSAKey() {
    echo "Generating OpenSSH server DSA (protocol version 2) key...\c"
    if $keyGenerator -q -t dsa -f $DSAKeyFile -N ''; then
        echo "done."
    else
        echo "failed!"
    fi
}


#
# Generates RSA (protocol version 2) key
#
generateRSA2Key() {
```

```
        echo "Generating OpenSSH server RSA (protocol version 2) key...\c"
        if $keyGenerator -q -t rsa -f $RSA2KeyFile -N ''; then
            echo "done."
        else
            echo "failed!"
        fi
}


#
# Generates RSA (protocol version 1) key
#
generateRSA1Key() {
        echo "Generating OpenSSH server RSA (protocol version 1) key...\c"
        if $keyGenerator -q -t rsa1 -f $RSA1KeyFile -N ''; then
            echo "done."
        else
            echo "failed!"
        fi
}


#
# Checks for keys and generates them if necessary
#
generateKeys() {
        if DSAKeyExists; then
            echo "OpenSSH DSA key exists: $DSAKeyFile"
        else
            generateDSAKey
        fi

        if RSA2KeyExists; then
            echo "OpenSSH RSA2 key exists: $RSA2KeyFile"
        else
            generateRSA2Key
        fi

        if RSA1KeyExists; then
            echo "OpenSSH RSA1 key exists: $RSA1KeyFile"
        else
            generateRSA1Key
        fi
}

#
# Checks for the seed file and generates one if necessary
#
generateSeed() {
        if [ "$usePRNGD" = "yes" ]; then
            if PRNGDSeedExists; then
```

```
                    echo "PRNGD seed exists: $PRNGDSeedFile"
            else
                    echo "Generating PRNGD initial seed file...\c"
                    touch $PRNGDSeedFile
                    chmod 600 $PRNGDSeedFile
                    # Newly installed system may not have log files
                    [ -s /var/adm/messages ] && \
                        cat /var/adm/messages >> $PRNGDSeedFile
                    [ -s /var/log/syslog ] && \
                        cat /var/log/syslog >> $PRNGDSeedFile
                    [ -s /var/cron/log ] && \
                        cat /var/cron/log >> $PRNGDSeedFile
                    ls -alni /proc >> $PRNGDSeedFile
                    ps -efly >> $PRNGDSeedFile
                    chmod 400 $PRNGDSeedFile
                    echo "done."
            fi
    fi
}


#
# Start the OpenSSH server process
#
startSSHD() {
    # check for configuration file
    if [ ! -f "$sshdConfig" ]; then
        echo "OpenSSH is not configured.  Missing file $sshdConfig."
        exit 1
    fi

    # check for all of the keys
    if DSAKeyExists && RSA2KeyExists && RSA1KeyExists; then
        :
    else
        generateKeys
    fi

    $sshdCmd $sshdCmdOptions
}

#
# Start the PRNGD process
#
startPRNGD() {
    if [ "$usePRNGD" = "yes" ]; then
        if PRNGDSeedExists; then
            :
        else
            generateSeed
```

```
            fi

        setPRNGDConfigFile

        # check that the directory containing the entropy pool exists
        [ ! -d $PRNGDEntropyDir ] && mkdir -p $PRNGDEntropyDir

        $PRNGDCmd $PRNGDCmdOptions
    fi
}

#
# Stop the OpenSSH server process
#
stopSSHD() {
    realPIDFile=""
    if [ -r "/etc/$sshdPIDFile" ]; then
        realPIDFile=/etc/$sshdPIDFile
    elif [ -r "/var/run/$sshdPIDFile" ]; then
        realPIDFile=/var/run/$sshdPIDFile
    else
        echo "OpenSSH server process ID (PID) file cannot be located."
    fi

    [ -n "$realPIDFile" ] && kill -TERM `cat $realPIDFile`
}

#
# Stop the PRNGD process
#
stopPRNGD() {
    # PRNGD has its own built method to shutdown and save its seed
    $PRNGDCmd --kill $PRNGDEntropyPool > /dev/null 2>&1
}

#
# Parse command argument
#
case "$1" in
    'start')
        # start the PRNGD process first to gather entropy
        startPRNGD
        startSSHD
        ;;

    'stop')
        stopSSHD
        stopPRNGD
        ;;
```

```
    'restart')
        stopSSHD
        stopPRNGD

        startPRNGD
        startSSHD
        ;;

    'keygen')
        # start PRNGD because key generation requires it
        stopSSHD
        startPRNGD

        generateKeys
        stopPRNGD
        ;;

    'seedgen')
        generateSeed
        ;;

    *)
        echo "Usage: $0 { start | stop | restart | keygen | seedgen }"
        ;;

esac

exit 0
```

Code Example for Packaging Script

The packaging script in this section creates an OpenSSH Solaris package. After OpenSSH is compiled, use this script to create a Solaris package stream. This script has been updated to support OpenSSH 3.5p1. For further information, refer to the Sun BluePrints OnLine articles titled "Building and Deploying OpenSSH on the Solaris Operating Environment" and "Building OpenSSH—Tools and Tradeoffs."

The latest version of this script is available at the Sun BluePrints OnLine tools area:

```
http://www.sun.com/blueprints/tools/
```

Usage

Execute this script in the top-level OpenSSH source directory. If needed, copy the script to the OpenSSH source directory. After OpenSSH has been compiled, check the script variables listed in the script to verify the configuration for the environment in which OpenSSH is to be installed.

Note – This script borrows heavily from the Sun Enterprise™ Network Security Service (SENSS) `makepackage` script. This script uses the `openssh.server init` script, which is copied over and some of its contents are changed based on the variables set in this script.

Contact

For inquiries or feedback, contact `openssh_tools@sun.com`.

Packaging Script Sample

```ksh
#!/usr/bin/ksh
#

# --------------------------------------------------------------------
# User configuration variables
# --------------------------------------------------------------------


#
# Installation directory.
#
#  This should be a local directory on the systems that will install it.
#  If /opt is specified, the package name will be appended to the
#  install directory name (ie. /opt/OBSDssh).
#
#  The default value, if no argument is supplied on the command line, is
#  /opt.  Otherwise, the argument specified will be used.
#
#  The location for the config files ie sshd_config is pulled from
#  OpenSSH's config.status.
installDir=/opt
#installDir=/usr/local


#
# OpenSSH Solaris package name.
#
packageName=OBSDssh

#  Check for OpenSSH's config.status as configuration is read from there.
if [[ ! -f config.status ]]; then
    print "Unable to read OpenSSH's config.status."
    exit 1
fi
#
# Include the PRNGD tool and associate files.  (yes/no)
# Check OpenSSH's config.status for --with-prngd-socket
#
if grep "with-prngd-socket" config.status > /dev/null 2>&1; then
    includePRNGD=yes
else
    includePRNGD=no
fi


#
# PRNGD package location.  (PRNGD must already be compiled.)
#
```

```
PRNGDDir=../prngd-0.9.26

#
# Solaris system init script location.
#
initScript=../openssh.server

#
# Install ssh set-user-ID (SUID).  (yes/no)
#
if grep "disable-suid-ssh" config.status > /dev/null 2>&1; then
   installSSHSUID=no
else
   installSSHSUID=yes
fi


# --------------------------------------------------------------------
# No further user configuration should be required past this point.
# --------------------------------------------------------------------

PATH=/usr/bin:/usr/ccs/bin

# source/current directory
srcDir=$(pwd)

# build directory
buildDir=/tmp/$packageName/build

# package build directory
packageDir=/tmp/$packageName/package

# OpenSSH files final location
if [[ $installDir == "/opt" ]]; then
    openSSHDir=$installDir/$packageName
else
    openSSHDir=$installDir
fi

# Determine config file location based on config.status of OpenSSH.
# The returned value needs to be a path not a shell variable.
configDir=$( grep @sysconfdir@ config.status | cut -f3 -d, )

# determine which ssh permissions to use
if [[ $installSSHSUID == "yes" ]]; then
    sshMode=4755
else
    sshMode=0755
fi
```

```
# cleanup and process
print "Cleaning up any old build files..."
rm -rf $buildDir $packageDir
mkdir -p $buildDir $packageDir

# create build subdirectories
print "Creating build subdirectories..."
mkdir -p $buildDir/$openSSHDir/bin
mkdir -p $buildDir/$openSSHDir/docs/OpenSSH
mkdir -p $buildDir/$openSSHDir/libexec
mkdir -p $buildDir/$openSSHDir/man/cat1
mkdir -p $buildDir/$openSSHDir/man/cat8
mkdir -p $buildDir/$openSSHDir/sbin
mkdir -p $buildDir/$configDir
mkdir -p $buildDir/etc/init.d
mkdir -p $buildDir/etc/rc0.d
mkdir -p $buildDir/etc/rc1.d
mkdir -p $buildDir/etc/rc2.d
mkdir -p $buildDir/etc/rc3.d
mkdir -p $buildDir/etc/rcS.d
[[ $includePRNGD == "yes" ]] && {
    mkdir -p $buildDir/$openSSHDir/docs/PRNGD
    mkdir -p $buildDir/var/run
}

# copy OpenSSH executables
print "Copying OpenSSH client executables:\c"
dir=$buildDir/$openSSHDir/bin
for file in ssh scp sftp ssh-add ssh-agent ssh-keygen ssh-keyscan \
    ssh-keysign; do
    cp $file $dir
    strip $dir/$file
    chmod 755 $dir/$file
    print " $file\c"
done
print "."

# copy OpenSSH server executable
print "Copying OpenSSH server executable: \c"
file=sshd
dir=$buildDir/$openSSHDir/sbin
cp $file $dir
strip $dir/$file
chmod 755 $dir/$file
print " $file."

# copy OpenSSH sftp server executable
print "Copying OpenSSH libexec executables:\c"
```

```
dir=$buildDir/$openSSHDir/libexec
for file in ssh-rand-helper sftp-server; do
    cp $file $dir
    strip $dir/$file
    chmod 755 $dir/$file
    print " $file\c"
done
print "."

# install only the preformatted man pages since Solaris nroff does not
#   understand the BSD formatted ones
print "Copying OpenSSH user preformatted man pages:\c"
dir=$buildDir/$openSSHDir/man/cat1
for file in ssh.0 scp.0 sftp.0 ssh-add.0 ssh-keygen.0 ssh-agent.0 \
    ssh-keyscan.0 ssh-rand-helper.0 ssh-keysign.0; do
    cp $file $dir
    chmod 644 $dir/$file
    print " $file\c"
done
print "."

print "Copying OpenSSH admin preformatted man pages:\c"
dir=$buildDir/$openSSHDir/man/cat8
for file in sftp-server.0 sshd.0; do
    cp $file $dir
    chmod 644 $dir/$file
    print " $file\c"
done
print "."

# create symbolic links to slogin and associated man page
print "Creating symbolic links to slogin and slogin.0..."
( cd $buildDir/$openSSHDir/bin; ln -s ./ssh slogin )
( cd $buildDir/$openSSHDir/man/cat1; ln -s ./ssh.0 slogin.0 )

# copy over auxilary config files
#   (Note: The ssh_prng_cmds file is only necessary if PRNGD is not used
#    but it is included anyways.)
print "Copying OpenSSH config files:\c"
dir=$buildDir/$configDir
for file in ssh_prng_cmds; do
    cp $file $dir
    chmod 644 $dir/$file
    print " $file\c"
done
cp ssh_config.out $dir/ssh_config
cp sshd_config.out $dir/sshd_config
chmod 644 $dir/ssh_config $dir/sshd_config
print " ssh_config sshd_config."
```

```
# copy over, fix permissions and ownerships, and link up the system
#  init script
print "Copying and linking the OpenSSH system init script..."
cat $initScript | \
    sed  -e "s#%%configDir%%#$configDir#g"                    \
         -e "s#%%openSSHDir%%#$openSSHDir#g  "         \
         -e "s#%%includePRNGD%%#$includePRNGD#g    " \
      > $buildDir/etc/init.d/openssh.server

chmod 744 $buildDir/etc/init.d/openssh.server
ln $buildDir/etc/init.d/openssh.server \
    $buildDir/etc/rc3.d/S25openssh.server
ln $buildDir/etc/init.d/openssh.server \
    $buildDir/etc/rcS.d/K30openssh.server
ln $buildDir/etc/init.d/openssh.server \
    $buildDir/etc/rc0.d/K30openssh.server
ln $buildDir/etc/init.d/openssh.server \
    $buildDir/etc/rc1.d/K30openssh.server
ln $buildDir/etc/init.d/openssh.server \
    $buildDir/etc/rc2.d/K40openssh.server

# if PRNGD is used, copy over the exectuable and config files
[[ $includePRNGD == "yes" ]] && {
    print "Copying PRNGD Solaris specific config files..."
    cp $PRNGDDir/prngd $buildDir/$openSSHDir/sbin
    cp $PRNGDDir/contrib/Solaris-2.6/prngd.conf.solaris-26 \
       $buildDir/$configDir/prngd.conf-solaris-2.6
    cp $PRNGDDir/contrib/Solaris-7/prngd.conf.solaris-7 \
       $buildDir/$configDir/prngd.conf-solaris-2.7
}

# copy over documentation files for OpenSSH and PRNGD
print "Copying OpenSSH and PRNGD documentation files:\c"
dir=$buildDir/$openSSHDir/docs/OpenSSH
for file in CREDITS README LICENCE; do
    cp $file $dir
    chmod 644 $dir/$file
    print " $file\c"
done

[[ $includePRNGD == "yes" ]] && {
    cp $PRNGDDir/00README \
       $buildDir/$openSSHDir/docs/PRNGD/README
    chmod 644 $buildDir/$openSSHDir/docs/PRNGD/README
    print " README (PRNGD)\c"
}
print "."
```

```
# create a Solaris package prototype file
print "Creating the Solaris package prototype file..."
(
    cd $buildDir
    find . ! -name prototype | sort | pkgproto | \
        awk '
            { $5="root"; $6="other"; }
            $3 == "etc"{ $4="?"; $5="?"; $6="?"; }
            $3 == "etc/rc0.d"    { $4="?"; $5="?"; $6="?"; }
            $3 == "etc/rc1.d"    { $4="?"; $5="?"; $6="?"; }
            $3 == "etc/rc2.d"    { $4="?"; $5="?"; $6="?"; }
            $3 == "etc/rc3.d"    { $4="?"; $5="?"; $6="?"; }
            $3 == "etc/rcS.d"    { $4="?"; $5="?"; $6="?"; }
            $3 == "etc/init. d"    { $4="?"; $5="?"; $6="?"; }
            $3 == "etc/init.d/openssh.server  "    { $6="sys"; }
            $3 == "etc/prngd.conf-solaris-2.6  "    { $6="sys"; }
            $3 == "etc/prngd.conf-solaris-2.7  "    { $6="sys"; }
            $3 == "etc/ssh_config  "      { $6="sys"; }
            $3 == "etc/ssh_prng_cmds  "    { $6="sys"; }
            $3 == "etc/sshd_config  "      { $6="sys"; }
            $3 == "var "          { $4="?"; $5="?"; $6="?"; }
            $3 == "var/run "      { $4="?"; $5="?"; $6="?"; }
            $3 == "opt "          { $4="?"; $5="?"; $6="?"; }
            { print; }
            END { print "i pkginfo=info" }' > prototype.temp

    sed -e "s/bin\/ssh 0755/bin\/ssh $sshMode/" < prototype.temp \
        | grep -v prototype.temp > prototype
    rm -f prototype.temp
)

# create an info file
print "Creating the Solaris package pkginfo file..."
cat > $buildDir/info << __EOF__
PKG=$packageName
NAME=OpenSSH for Solaris
ARCH=$(uname -p)
VERSION="$(grep SSH_VERSION $srcDir/version.h | sed -e 's/.*_\([0-9]\)/\1/g')"
CATEGORY=application
BASEDIR=/
CLASSES="none"
__EOF__

# make a package, using the prototype/info files, writing to the scratchdir
print "Creating the Solaris package directory..."
pkgmk -d $packageDir -f $buildDir/prototype -r $buildDir -o

# store it as Solaris package stream format
print "Creating the Solaris package stream."
```

```
pkgtrans -os $packageDir $srcDir/$packageName.pkg all

# messages
print
print "Package stream file is: $srcDir/$packageName.pkg"
print "To install: pkgadd -d $packageName.pkg $packageName"

# done
exit 0
```

Code Example for PRNGD Sanity Check

The following is an example of a simple sanity check of PRNGD:

```
/* Simple sanity check of PRNGD */
/* Open a UNIX socket, requests four bytes of data. */
/* Displays the data and closes the socket. */
/* EGD protocol from egd.pl out of egd-08.tar.gz */
/*      Send messages over the entropy pool (an UNIX socket.)
Get entropy level
        Send        0x00
        Response    Four bytes 0xaa 0xbb 0xcc 0xdd aa is the MSB and dd LSB.
Read entropy non-blocking
        Send        0x01 0xnn where nn is the number of bytes requested.
        Response     0xmm <data> where mm is the number of bytes transmitted.
Read entropy blocking
        Send        0x02 0xnn where nn is the number of bytes requested.
        Response     <data> nn bytes. PRNGD will block if not available.
Write entropy
        Send        0x03 0xaa 0xbb 0xnn <data>
                         aa and bb are the bits of entropy, nn is
                         the number of bytes of data.
        Response
Get PID of PRNGD
        Send        0x04
        Response     0xmm <data> where mm is the number of bytes transmitted.
                         Receive a non null-terminated PID string.

*/


#include <stdio.h>
#include <stdlib.h>
#include <sys/types.h>
```

```
#include <sys/socket.h>
#include <string.h>
#include <sys/un.h>
#include <unistd.h>

int main(int argc, char *argv[])
{
        int n, s, len;
        char buf[1];
        char command[2];
        struct sockaddr_un name;

        if (argc != 2)
        {
                fprintf (stderr,"Usage: %s <prngd pool>\n",argv[0]);
                exit(1);
        }

        if ((s = socket(AF_UNIX, SOCK_STREAM, 0)) < 0)
        {
                perror("socket");
                exit(1);
        }

        memset(&name, 0, sizeof(struct sockaddr_un));

        name.sun_family = AF_UNIX;
        strncpy(name.sun_path, argv[1], sizeof(name.sun_path));
        len=sizeof(name.sun_family) + sizeof(name.sun_path);

        if (connect(s, (struct sockaddr *) &name, len) < 0)
        {
                perror("connect");
                exit(1);
        }

        /* send message requesting four bytes non blocking*/
        command[0] = 0x01;
        command[1] = 0x04;
        if (send(s, command, sizeof(command), 0) < 0)
        {
                perror("send");
                exit(1);
        }

        /* receive response */
        /* get the amount bytes being received */
        if ((n = recv(s, buf, sizeof(buf), 0)) > 0)
        {
```

```
                len=(int)buf[0];
        } else {
                perror("recv");
                exit(1);
        }

        /* receive and display the data */
        while ((len > 0) && ((n = recv(s, buf, sizeof(buf), 0)) > 0))
        {
                fprintf(stdout, "%d ", (int)buf[0]);
                len--;
        }
        fprintf(stdout,"\n");

        close(s);
        return 0;
}
```

Server Configuration Files

This section contains examples of server configuration files that you can use in your environment.

DMZ-Bastion Host Server

The following is an example of the DMZ-bastion host server Secure Shell configuration file:

```
# Protocol and server operation
Compression yes
KeepAlive yes
MaxStartups 10
HostKey /etc/ssh/ssh_host_rsa_key
HostKey /etc/ssh/ssh_host_dsa_key
Protocol 2
Port 22
# If using OpenSSH
UseLogin no
UsePrivilegeSeparation no

# Authentication
# Only allow public key based authentication. No passwords.
```

```
DSAAuthentication yes
LoginGraceTime 60
PAMAuthenticationViaKBDInt yes
PasswordAuthentication no
PermitEmptyPasswords no
PermitRootLogin no
PubKeyAuthentication yes

# User environment
AllowTCPForwarding no
Banner /etc/issue
CheckMail no
GatewayPorts no
PrintMotd no
StrictModes yes
X11Forwarding no
```

Legacy Support

The following is an example of the Secure Shell server configuration file with legacy support.

```
# Protocol and server operation
Compression yes
KeepAlive yes
MaxStartups 10
HostKey /etc/ssh/ssh_host_rsa_key
HostKey /etc/ssh/ssh_host_dsa_key
# Enable protocol 1 but default to protocol 2.
Protocol 2,1
Port 22
# If using OpenSSH
UseLogin no
UsePrivilegeSeparation no

# Authentication
DSAAuthentication yes
LoginGraceTime 60
PAMAuthenticationViaKBDInt yes
PasswordAuthentication yes
PermitEmptyPasswords no
PermitRootLogin no
PubKeyAuthentication yes

# User environment
AllowTCPForwarding yes
```

```
Banner /etc/issue
CheckMail no
GatewayPorts no
PrintMotd no
StrictModes yes
X11DisplayOffset 10
X11Forwarding yes
XAuthLocation /usr/X/bin/xauth

# Legacy support options - protocol 1
HostKey /etc/ssh/ssh_host_key
IgnoreRhosts yes
IgnoreUserKnownHosts yes
KeyRegenerationInterval 1800
RhostsAuthentication no
RhostsRSAAuthentication no
```

Workstation Server

The following is an example of the Secure Shell workstation server configuration file:

```
# Protocol and server operation
Compression yes
KeepAlive yes
MaxStartups 10
HostKey /etc/ssh/ssh_host_rsa_key
HostKey /etc/ssh/ssh_host_dsa_key
Protocol 2
Port 22
# If using OpenSSH
UseLogin no
UsePrivilegeSeparation no

# Authentication
DSAAuthentication yes
LoginGraceTime 60
PAMAuthenticationViaKBDInt yes
PasswordAuthentication yes
PermitEmptyPasswords no
PermitRootLogin no
PubKeyAuthentication yes

# User environment
AllowTCPForwarding yes
Banner /etc/issue
CheckMail no
```

```
GatewayPorts no
PrintMotd no
StrictModes yes
X11DisplayOffset 10
X11Forwarding yes
XAuthLocation /usr/X/bin/xauth
```

Client Configurations

This section contains examples of the client configuration files for remote workers and client workstations.

Remote Worker Configuration File

The following is an example of the Secure Shell user configuration file for remote workers.

```
# nickname for bastion host
Host work
        Hostname dmz.someplace.com
        Port 2929
        User max

# Defaults - must login via an identity key using only protocol 2.
Host *
        CheckHostIP yes
        Compression yes
        CompressionLevel 9
        ConnectionAttempts 3
        DSAAuthentication yes
        FallBackToRsh no
        ForwardAgent no
        ForwardX11 yes
        GatewayPorts no
        KeepAlive yes
        LocalForward 8080 intranet.extremefoosticks.com:80
        PasswordAuthentication no
        Protocol 2
        PubkeyAuthentication  yes
        RhostsAuthentication no
        RhostsRSAAuthentication no
        RSAAuthentication no
```

```
StrictHostKeyChecking  yes
UsePrivilegedPort no
UseRsh no
XAuthLocation /usr/X/bin/xauth
```

Workstation Configuration File

The following is an example of the Secure Shell user configuration file for a workstation.

```
# nickname for remote server
Host server
       HostName server.faroff.corp

# remote host needing a network proxy to access.
Host remote
       HostName remote.otherplace.org
       User pablo
       ProxyCommand /usr/lib/ssh/ssh-socks5-proxy-connect -h socks.server
-p 1080 remote.otherplace.org 22

# Defaults
Host *
       CheckHostIP yes
       Compression yes
       CompressionLevel 6
       FallBackToRsh no
       ForwardAgent no
       ForwardX11 yes
       GatewayPorts no
       KeepAlive yes
       PasswordAuthentication yes
       Protocol 2
       StrictHostKeyChecking ask
       UseRsh no
       XAuthLocation /usr/X/bin/xauth
```

Resources

This appendix contains lists of resources that provide further information on the topics discussed in this book.

Solaris Secure Shell Software Documentation

The following man pages are installed as part of the SUNWman package:

- scp(1)
- sftp(1)
- sftp-server(1M)
- ssh(1)
- ssh-add(1)
- ssh-agent(1)
- ssh-http-proxy-connect(1)
- ssh-keygen(1)
- ssh-socks5-proxy-connect(1)
- ssh_config(4)
- sshd(1M)
- sshd_config(4)

Additional information can be found in *System Administrator Guide: Security Services* in the Solaris 9 System Administration Collection on docs.sun.com.

OpenSSH Documentation

The following man pages are shipped with the software source:

- scp(1)
- ssh-add(1)
- ssh-keyscan(1)
- ssh(1)
- sftp(1)
- ssh-agent(1)
- ssh-keysign(1)
- slogin(1)
- ssh-keygen(1)
- ssh-rand-helper(1)
- sftp-server(8)
- sshd(8)

Additional documentation can be found at the OpenSSH Web site:
www.openssh.com

Software

- Usenet newsgroups archive: http://groups.google.com
- Mailing ARChive archives: http://marc.theaimsgroup.com/
- Request for comments (RFC): http://www.ietf.org/rfc.html
- Prebuilt versions of the software (except the Sun ONE Studio software): http://www.sunfreeware.com/
- GNU compiler collection
  - Web site: http://www.fsf.org/software/gcc/gcc.html
  - Frequently asked questions: http://www.fsf.org/software/gcc/faq.html
  - Documentation: http://www.fsf.org/software/gcc/onlinedocs/
  - Subscription details: http://www.fsf.org/software/gcc/lists.html

- Mailing lists:
  `gcc-announce@gcc.gnu.org` (announcements of new releases)
  `gcc-help@gcc.gnu.org` (help forum)
- Usenet newsgroups:
  `gnu.gcc`
  `gnu.gcc.announce`
  `gnu.gcc.bug`
  `gnu.gcc.help`
- GNU privacy guard
  - Web site: `http://www.gnupg.org/`
  - Frequently asked questions: `http://www.gnupg.org/faq.html`
  - Subscription details: `http://www.gnupg.org/docs-mls.html`
  - Mailing lists:
    `announce@gnupg.org` (announcements of new releases)
    `gnupg-users@gnupg.org` (discussion and help forum)
  - Usenet newsgroup: `comp.security.pgp`
  - RFC 2240
- Gzip
  - Web site: `http://www.gzip.org/`
    See also Zlib.
- OpenSSL
  - Web site: `http://www.openssl.org/`
  - Frequently asked questions: `http://www.openssl.org/support/faq.cgi`
  - Subscription details: `http://www.openssl.org/support/`
  - Mailing lists:
    `openssl-announce@openssl.org` (announcements of new releases)
    `openssl-users@openssl.org` (discussion and help forum)
  - Usenet newsgroup: `sci.crypt`
- OpenSSH
  - Web site: `http://www.openssh.com`
  - Frequently asked questions: `http://www.openssh.com/faq.html`
  - Subscription details: `http://www.openssh.com/list.html`
  - Mailing lists:
    `openssh-unix-announce@mindrot.org` (announcements of new releases)
    `secureshell@securityfocus.com` (discussion and help forum)
  - Usenet newsgroups: `comp.security.ssh`
- Perl
  - Web site: `http://www.perl.com/`

- Documentation: `http://www.perldoc.com/`
- Mailing lists: `http://lists.perl.org/`
- Usenet newsgroups:
  `comp.lang.perl`
  `comp.lang.perl.announce`
- PRNGD
  - Web site: `http://ftp.aet.TU-Cottbus.DE/personen/jaenicke/postfix_tls/prngd.html`
  - Usenet newsgroups:
    `sci.math.stat`
    `sci.stat`
- Sun ONE Studio Compiler Collection (formerly the Forte Compiler Collection)
  - Web site: `http://forte.sun.com/s1scc/index.html`
  - Documentation: `http://docs.sun.com/`
  - Frequently asked questions:
    `http://www.sun.com/software/sundev/suncc/faqs/index.html`
- TCP Wrappers
  - Web site: `ftp://ftp.porcupine.org/pub/security/index.html`
- Zlib
  - Web site: `http://www.gzip.org/zlib/`
  - Documentation: `http://www.gzip.org/zlib/manual.html`
  - Frequently asked questions for Zlib:
    `http://www.gzip.org/zlib/zlib_faq.html`
  - Frequently asked questions for Comp.compression:
    `http://www.faqs.org/faqs/compression-faq/`
  - Subscription details:
    `http://zlib.net/mailman/listinfo/zlib-announce_madler.net`
  - Mailing list: `Zlib-announce@zlib.org`
  - Usenet newsgroup: `comp.compression`
  - RFC 1950, 1951, 1952

Bibliography

This bibliography contains a list of the books, articles, and other reference material used in *Secure Shell in the Enterprise*.

Sun BluePrints OnLine Articles

These articles are available on the Sun BluePrints OnLine CD or at the Sun BluePrints OnLine web site: `http://www.sun.com/blueprints/`

- Cockcroft, Adrian. "Observability." December 1999.

- ——. "Processing Accounting Data into Workloads." October 1999.

- ——. "Scenario Planning - Part 1," February 2000.

- ——. "Scenario Planning - Part 2," March 2000.

- Dasan, Vasanthan, Alex Noordergraaf, and Lou Ordorica. "The Solaris Fingerprint Database - A Security Tool for Solaris Operating Environment Files." May 2001.

- Elling, Richard. "Static Performance Tuning." May 2000.

- Englund, Martin. "Securing Systems with Host-Based Firewalls." September 2001.

- Haines, Michael, and Joep Vesseur. "Extending Authentication in the Solaris 9 Operating Environment Using Pluggable Authentication Modules (PAM): Part I." September 2002.

- ——. "Extending Authentication in the Solaris 9 Operating Environment Using Pluggable Authentication Modules (PAM): Part II." October 2002.

- Hill, Jon, and Kemer Thomson. "System Performance Management Moving from Chaos to Value." July 2001.

- Howard, John, and Alex Noordergraaf. "WebStart Flash." November 2001.

- Ingersoll, Wyllys. "Kerberos Network Security in the Solaris Operating Environment." October 2001.

- Lindh, Börje. "Application Performance Optimization." March 2002.
- Martin, Jean-Christophe. "Policy-Based Networks." October 1999.
- McDougall, Richard. "Availability - What It Means, Why It's Important, and How to Improve It." October 1999.
- Nguyen, John. "Establishing an Architectural Model." February 2002.
- Noordergraaf, Alex. "How Hackers Do It: Tricks, Tools, and Techniques." May 2002.
- ——. "Building Secure N-tier Environments." October 2002.
- Noordergraaf, Alex, and Glen Brunette. "The Solaris Security Toolkit—Quick Start: Update for the version 0.3." June 2001.
- Osser, William, and Alex Noordergraaf. "Auditing in the Solaris 8 Operating Environment." February 2001.
- Reid, Jason. "Configuring OpenSSH for the Solaris Operating Environment." January 2002.
- Reid, Jason, and Keith Watson. "Building and Deploying OpenSSH for the Solaris Operating Environment." July 2001.
- Stringfellow, Stan. "Architecting a Service Provider Infrastructure for Maximum Growth." June 2000.
- Sun Microsystems, Inc. "Operating Environments: Building Longevity into Solaris Operating Environment Applications." April 2000.
- Weise, Joel. "Public Key Infrastructure." August 2001.
- Weise, Joel, and Charles R. Martin. "Developing a Security Policy." December 2001.

External Articles

- BJN. "VPN Howto." October 1999.
  http://www.defcon1.org/html/ssh/vpn-howto/vpn-howto.html
- Huey, Benjamin. "Penetration Testing on 80211b Networks." SANS Institute: Information Security Reading Room. February 2002.
  http://rr.sans.org/wireless/test_80211b.php
- Kaminsky, Dan. "Advanced OpenSSH." April 2002.
  http://www.doxpara.com/Advanced_OpenSSH.pdf
- McGraw, Gary, and John Viega. "Make your software behave: Playing the numbers." IBM developerWorks. April 2000.
  http://www.ibm.com/software/developer/library/playing/index.html

- ——. "Make your software behave: Beating the bias." IBM developerWorks. April 2000.
  `http://www.ibm.com/software/developer/library/beating.html`
- ——. "Make your software behave: Software Strategies." IBM developerWorks. April 2000.
  `http://www.ibm.com/software/developer/library/beating.html`
- Meredith, Gayle. "Securing the Wireless LAN." *Packet Magazine*. July 2001.
  `http://www.cisco.com/warp/public/784/packet/jul01/p74-cover.html`
- Robbins, Daniel. "OpenSSH Key Management: Understanding RSA/DSA Authentication." IBM developerworks. July 2001.
- ——. "OpenSSH Key Management: Introducing ssh-agent and keychain." IBM developerworks. September 2001.
- ——. "OpenSSH Key Management: Agent Forwarding and keychain improvements." IBM developerworks. February 2002.
- RSA Security, Inc. "Factorization of RSA-155."
  `http://www.rsasecurity.com/rsalabs/challenges/factoring/rsa155.html`
- Rudich, Joe. "IPSec Simplified." IBM developerworks. April 2001.
  `http://www.ibm.com/developerworks/library/s-ipsec.html`
- Starkey, M. L. "Getting Started with the latest PPP Software from Sun Microsystems." November 2002.
  `http://www.stokely.com/unix.serial.port.resources/starkey.html`
- Sun Microsystems, Inc. "IPSec in the Solaris 9 Operating Environment: A Technical White Paper." Sun Microsystems. 2002.
  `http://wwws.sun.com/software/whitepapers/solaris9/ipsec.pdf`

Books

- Anderson, Ross. *Security Engineering A Guide to Building Dependable Distributed Systems*. New York: Wiley Computer Publishing, 2001.
- Barrett, Daniel J., and Richard E. Silverman. *SSH: The Secure Shell*. Sebastopol, CA: O'Reilly, 2001.
- Black, Uyless. *Data Networks Concepts, Theory, and Practice*. Englewood Cliffs, NJ: Prentice-Hall, 1989.
- Cordingly, David. *Under the Black Flag*. Fort Washington, PA: Harvest Books, 1997.
- Denning, Dorothy Elizabeth Robling. *Cryptography and Data Security*. Reading, MA: Addison-Wesley, 1982.
- Frisch, Aeleen. *Essential System Administration Second Edition*. Sebastopol, CA: O'Reilly, 1995.

- Garfinkel, Simson, and Gene Spafford. *Practical Unix and Internet Security, Second Edition*. Sebastopol, CA: O'Reilly, 1996.

- Howard, John, and Alex Noordergraaf. *JumpStart Technology Effective Use in the Solaris Operating Environment*. Palo Alto, CA: Sun Microsystems Press, 2002.

- Hughes, Jr., Larry J. *Actually Useful Internet Security Techniques*. Indianapolis, IN: New Riders Publishing, 1995.

- Noordergraaf, Alex, and Glen Brunette. *Securing Systems with the Solaris Security Toolkit*. Palo Alto, CA: Sun Microsystems Press, 2003.

- Olczak, Anatole. *The Korn Shell: User and Programming Manual*. Revised Edition. Reading, MA: Addison Wesley, 1997.

- Robbins, Kay A., and Steven Robbins. *Practical Unix Programming A Guide to Concurrency, Communication, and Multithreading*. Englewood Cliffs, NJ: Prentice-Hall, 1996.

- Salus, Peter H. *Casting the Net*. Reading, MA: Addison-Wesley, 1995.

- Schneier, Bruce. *Applied Cryptography Protocols, Algorithms, and Source Code in C*. New York: Wiley, 1994.

- Silberschatz, Abraham, and Peter B. Galvin. *Operating System Concepts, Fourth Edition*. Reading, MA: Addison-Wesley, 1994.

- Singh, Simon. *The Code Book*. New York: First Anchor Books, 1999.

- Stern, Hal. *Managing NFS and NIS*. Sebastopol, CA: O'Reilly, 1991.

- Stinson, Douglas R. *Cryptography Theory and Practice*, CRC Press, 1995.

- Sun Microsystems, Inc. *Solaris 9 System Administration Guide: Resource Management and Network Services*, Solaris 9 System Administration Collection. Palo Alto: Sun Microsystems, Inc., 2002.

- ——. *Solaris 9 System Administration Guide: Security Services*, Solaris 9 System Administration Collection. Palo Alto: Sun Microsystems, Inc., 2002.

- SunSoft™ Alliance Developer Engineering. *Solaris Porting Guide: Second Edition*. Mountain View: SunSoft Press, 1995.

- Van Der Lubbe, Jan C. A. *Basic Methods of Cryptography*. Cambridge: Cambridge University Press, 1998.

- Winkler, Ira. *Corporate Espionage: What it is, Why it is happening in your company, and what you must do about it*. New York: Prima Publishing, 1999.

Bug Reports

- Bug 2 filed by Darren Moffat in the Portable OpenSSH bugzilla system at
  `http://bugzilla.mindrot.org/show_bug.cgi?id=2`
- Bug 125 filed by Andrew Sydelko in the Portable OpenSSH bugzilla system at
  `http://bugzilla.mindrot.org/show_bug.cgi?id=125`

FAQs

- Hornstein, Ken. "`comp.protocols.kerberos` Frequently Asked Questions."
  United States Government. 2000.
  `http://www.nrl.navy.mil/CCS/people/kenh/kerberos-faq.html`
- Miller, Todd. "SUDO." 2002. `http://www.courtesan.com/sudo/`
- Muffet, Alec. "Frequently Asked Questions for Crack v5.0a." 1999.
  `http://www.users.dircon.co.uk/~crypto/download/c50-faq.html`
- Powell, Brad, Dan Farmer, and Matthew Archibald. "Titan Frequently Asked
  Questions." 2002.
  `http://www.fish.com/titan/FAQ.html`
- OpenBSD Group. "OpenSSH Frequently Asked Questions." April 2002.
  `http://www.openssh.com/faq.html`
- RSA Laboratories. "Frequently Asked Questions about Today's Cryptography."
  Version 4.1. RSA Security, Inc.
  `http://www.rsasecurity.com/rsalabs/faq/index.html`

Man Pages

- `ssh(1)`
- `ssh_config(1)`
- `sshd_config(1)`
- `ssh_config` (OpenSSH 3.5p1)
- `sshd_config` (OpenSSH 3.5p1)
- `pppd(1M)`

Presentations

- Borisov, Nikita, Ian Goldberg, and David Wagner. "Intercepting Mobile Communications: The Insecurity of 802.11." 7th Annual International Conference on Mobile Computing and Networking. http://www.isaac.cs.berkeley.edu/isaac/mobicom.pdf

- Dio, Surinder. "Summary: Proving OpenSSH 3.4p1 is using /dev/urandom (Solaris 9 ossh Vs OpenBSD ossh)." Posted to focus-sun@securityfocus.com. July 23, 2002.

- Muffet, Alec, and Jason Carolan. "Service Delivery Network: A Modern 'Defense-In-Depth' approach to Security." Sun Network Conference. September 2002

- Watson, Keith. "The Solaris Operating Environment, OpenSSH, and PRNGs." Sun Microsystems, Inc. Usenix BOF Presentation.

Security Information

The following *Free Info Docs* are available by searching on the document number on the SunSolve Web site: http://sunsolve.sun.com

- "Learn BSM/C2/SunShield in 5 minutes," 27064
- "How do I configure TCP Wrappers in Solaris 9 Operating Environment," 51322
- "RBAC: Creating A Role," 25968

Index

B

background jobs, 60
bandwidth
    amount consumed, 64
    file transfers, 92
    performance, 91
    Secure Shell consumption, 92
    sizing, 98
banner, 46, 129
Basic Security Module, 15, 45, 81
bastion host, 47
Berkeley r-commands, 12
Berkeley r-protocols, 59
Blowfish, 5, 93, 144
Bourne shell, 76
BSM, 108
BSM auditing, 48
build-time configuration, 42
build-time costs, 22

C

C shell, 76
CAPP, 81
ciphers, 93, 111, 130, 144
class events, 85
client
    options, 143
    usage, 113
comments in configuration files, 42
Common Desktop Environment, 77
compilation, 37
compilers, 23
compression, 44, 50, 130, 144
compromised credentials, 62
confidentiality, 2, 5
config script, 35
configuration
    client, 42
    client options, 143
    examples, 54
    options, 49
    order of precedence, 41

server, 42
server options, 127
configuration files
    client, 42, 121, 179
    comments, 42
    custom, 57
    default, 54
    global client, 42
    keyword-value pairs, 42
    OpenSSH, 38
    options, 42
    server, 42, 176
    server locations, 123
    workstation, 178, 180
Configure Perl script, 35
connection attempts, 145
cryptographic elements
    algorithms, 35
    hash, 27
    hash functions, 6
    keys, 26
    operations, 75
    protocols, 5, 7, 18
cryptography, 4, 5, 71
cyclic redundancy checks, 4

D

debugging, 110
defend-in-depth, 41
denial of service, 34
deployment, 55
destination host, 116, 148, 151
determination attacks, 150
distribute hosts keys, 51
distribution, 53
DMZ-bastion host, 176
domain name service, 72, 97
    spoofing, 143
downed connections, 50
DSA
    authentication, 131, 132, 145
    identities, 95
    identity file, 148

MD5
  hashes, 55
  integrity, 4
  key fingerprint, 73
  signatures, 58
  software, 21
message
  authentication algorithm, 149
  authentication code, 134
message-of-the-day, 46, 109, 138
metacluster, 56
metaclusters, 22
minimized installations, 57
misconfiguration, 41
MPEG2, 144
multihomed machines, 133
multiple forwards, 68

N

naming scheme, 75
Netscape, 16
network
  accessible hosts, 101
  connections, 159
  interface, 44
  stack, 2
NFS, 74
  timeouts, 98
NIS, 97
  environments, 47
non-interactive sessions, 87

O

offline factoring, 49
Open Directory Project, 16
OpenBSD, 15, 19
OpenSSH, 15
  arguments, 37
  building, 19
  compilation, 37
  configuration files, 38
  configuring, 37

  message-of-the-day, 46
  resources, 183
OpenSSH Solaris package, 166
openssh.server script, 54
OpenSSL, 35
  architectures, 35
  resources, 183
options
  configuration, 49
  global defaults, 49
OS upgrades, 111

P

packages, 53
  installation, 159
  script, 54
packet insertion, 138, 150
PalmOS, 15
PAM, 136
passphrase-free logins, 74
passphrases, 3, 60, 73, 77, 143
password-free logins, 48, 51
passwords, 3
  auditing, 89
  authentication, 136
  empty, 45
  length, 138
  problems, 73
  prompting, 143, 149
  ssh(1M), 60
  user file permissions, 48
  user identities, 51
patches, 23, 87, 111
  OpenSSH, 110
  Solaris OE, 110
performance, 44, 81, 91, 144, 155
Perl, 24, 183
permission denied error, 60
pluggable authentication modules, 37, 45
ports, 47
  forwarding, 68, 118, 128, 131, 140, 147
  scanning, 33
PPP, 101

technical support
  OpenSSH, 109
  Solaris Secure Shell software, 109
Telnet
  command, 61
  local forwarding, 119
  replacement, 12
  service, 70
  unsafe commands, 10
terminal windows, 77
transparency, 68
tunneling, 46
two-factor authentication, 2, 45

U

UIDs, 72, 128
unauthenticated connections, 135
unencrypted
  identities, 62
  private key, 79
unprivileged
  processes, 140
  users, 46
urandom, 27
usage
  client, 113
  server, 122
UseLogin, 48
user
  environment, 43
  identities, 62
  IDs, 82

V

variables
  eval(1M), 118
  script, 167
  shell, 107
verbosity, 89, 149
version string, 111

virtual private networks, 11
  forwarded ports, 131
  protocol, 5
  tools, 9

W

Web traffic, 8
WebNFS, 12, 92
  mounts, 69
WebStart Flash, 54
wildcards, 107

X

X
  connections, 46
  daemon, 111
  forwarding, 47, 87, 113, 120
X11
  applications, 141
  forwarding, 140, 146
  servers, 141
  sessions, 19

Z

Zlib, 24, 56, 184

http://www.phptr.com/

Prentice Hall PTR   InformIT   InformIT Online Books   Financial Times Prentice Hall   ft.com   PTG Interactive   Reuters

TOMORROW'S SOLUTIONS FOR TODAY'S PROFESSIONALS

Prentice Hall **Professional Technical Reference**

| Browse | Book Series | What's New | User Groups | Alliances | Special Sales | Contact Us |

Search | Help | Home

Quick Search

PTR Favorites

Find a Bookstore

Book Series

Special Interests

Newsletters

Press Room

International

Best Sellers

Solutions Beyond the Book

Shopping Bag

Keep Up to Date with
PH PTR Online

We strive to stay on the cutting edge of what's happening in professional computer science and engineering. Here's a bit of what you'll find when you stop by **www.phptr.com**:

What's new at PHPTR? We don't just publish books for the professional community, we're a part of it. Check out our convention schedule, keep up with your favorite authors, and get the latest reviews and press releases on topics of interest to you.

Special interest areas offering our latest books, book series, features of the month, related links, and other useful information to help you get the job done.

User Groups Prentice Hall Professional Technical Reference's User Group Program helps volunteer, not-for-profit user groups provide their members with training and information about cutting-edge technology.

Companion Websites Our Companion Websites provide valuable solutions beyond the book. Here you can download the source code, get updates and corrections, chat with other users and the author about the book, or discover links to other websites on this topic.

Need to find a bookstore? Chances are, there's a bookseller near you that carries a broad selection of PTR titles. Locate a Magnet bookstore near you at www.phptr.com.

Subscribe today! Join PHPTR's monthly email newsletter! Want to be kept up-to-date on your area of interest? Choose a targeted category on our website, and we'll keep you informed of the latest PHPTR products, author events, reviews and conferences in your interest area.

Visit our mailroom to subscribe today! **http://www.phptr.com/mail_lists**